THAT'S THE

Spirit!

The Lighter Side of Life in Wartime Britain

Derek French

Cover image, and interior watercolour illustrations by:
Shelagh Armstrong

Images on pages: 33, 37, 60, 62, 174, 238, 262, 270, 286, 298 accessed courtesy of Wikimedia Commons.

All other photographs in possession of the author.

ISBN-10: 1727692187
ISBN- 13: 978-1727692181

Chapters

Acknowledgements

I had help ...

The first thank you should go to my parents. My father and mother decided to have a large family, of which I was the youngest of seven children. Some would say that I was an after-thought as I was born five years after my next youngest sibling. Others might have another explanation! Whatever the cause, my parents provided me with a lot of material about which to write.

From the straight-ahead, traditional style of the eldest in the family, to the wild antics of my red-haired sister, and to the Irish traits of my suitably named brother called Mick, there was a cornucopia of good material about which to write. So, thanks go first to my Mum and Dad. Bless 'em. Continuing along family lines, my thanks go to one of my grandchildren, Nicholas Harrison. Despite a busy workload at his university, Nick has devoted many hours helping to edit the manuscript and tracking down suitable wartime photographs to make the narrative come alive. As with many authors of a certain age, navigating the modern digital world calls for a younger brain to bring this book from mere ideas to the printed form. Nick was always there to make it all happen.

For the editing help at an early stage and enthusiastic support to keep my work ethic from flagging, I am indebted to Jane Thornton. Thank you Jane, for keeping my spirits up and providing me with the conviction that at least some people will want to read the final result. Contributing to the light touch which I have been seeking, my thanks go to Shelagh Armstrong and Paul Hodgson for the illustrations and cover design. Their patience was endless with the "what ifs" of my vacillating mind.

Finally, I owe a huge thank you to my dear wife, Bobbie. She has endured endless hours of my less than holy language as I have struggled with my ineptitude on the computer and other modern digital equipment. Despite my antisocial behaviour, she has maintained her conviction that there has always been a light at the end of the tunnel; that the end has justified the means.

I thank you all.

Introduction

I am calling this an *Introduction* but perhaps a better term would be an *Explanation*, or even a *Justification*. In some ways, perhaps I should call it an *Apology*.

What I have written is part memoir and part history, with an unavoidably good dose of bias. It all takes place in the years of 1939 to 1945, with a few extra comments about those dreary years following the end of the war. Many books have been written about these tumultuous years and it is presumptuous of me to add my experiences and memories to this well-documented era. However, I believe I offer a perspective which, while hardly unique, does open a window on the interesting times experienced by an impressionable youth.

First, I would ask you to consider my age during WWII. I was six years and six months old when war was declared. I was twelve years and three months old on VE Day. That is nearly six years of experience at a very formative age. I was old enough to remember it all but too young to fully comprehend the true nature of the war's horror. You could say I was able to view events with the innocence of youth, but that is an over simplification, and far too grand a statement for the experiences of a scruffy kid getting by day-to-day in a world in which adults had more important things to do than pay much attention to young people like me.

Here is the second reason why I feel compelled to record my experiences: my family lived about 25 miles south east of London, just south of the River Thames. This placed us directly on one of the most favoured lines of flight for the Luftwaffe on their way to the primary target of London. Both by day and night, the ribbon of the Thames estuary was like a road map for the German pilots. From this location, we had a ringside seat on the unfolding drama. We were surrounded by R.A.F. bases which gave us a first-hand view of the aerial battles during the Battle of Britain. In 1944, we were centrally located in Doodlebug Alley when Hitler's V1's droned their way across the sky. The most satisfying event took place on D-Day when the Allied air armada woke us up as the skies were filled with aircraft from horizon to horizon. To put it succinctly, my home was located under the thick of the action.

My third reason for putting pen to paper is that I am fortunate to have been raised on a farm which gave my family various advantages. We could put food on the table at all times despite the restrictions of the food ration book. In addition, our countryside location gave us more exposure to the various actions and events involved in the waging of war compared to my cohorts who were confined to living in a more restricted urban situation where the view was limited to their streetscape.

My age, where I lived, and the advantages of life on the farm provided me with a unique set of circumstances. In short, I was a very lucky fellow, and I appreciate the chances of fate which put me in this position. Happily, this good fortune followed me throughout my life.

This is the reason I considered calling this an *Apology* rather than an *Introduction*. I am well aware that for many boys of my age–and their families–the wartime experience was hell on earth. That I managed to avoid the horrors of the war makes me feel somewhat guilty. But I can only record what I remember, and if some of my experiences have been treated in a light-hearted manner I do apologize to those of my readers for whom their experiences were of a different and more serious nature.

All war is infinitely more horrifying than anything that can be put on paper. If you, Dear Reader, recall WWII in very different terms I hope you will forgive me and realize that this is a tale of wartime experiences as seen through the eyes of a very fortunate boy.

Derek French

War Is Declared

There was always hope but, as time went by, the chances of avoiding war diminished.

The steady downslope to the conflict with Germany can be traced back to 1935. At that time, Ramsay MacDonald of Britain, Pierre Laval of France, and Benito Mussolini of Italy met on the beautiful little island of Isola Bella on Lake Maggiore in Italy. I had the pleasure of visiting the island in the 1980's and it is truly beautiful. They met to form an alliance opposing the rearmament of Germany and the annexation of Austria by Hitler. Such moves by Germany would have been in direct conflict with the Treaty of Versailles which marked the end of World War One in 1918.

At the meeting's conclusion, the trio signed "The Declaration of Stresa". It is named after the town on the southern shores of Lake Maggiore. The agreement was short lived as later in 1935 Mussolini invaded Abyssinia (Ethiopia) against the wishes of Britain and France who had colonies bordering on this country. The declaration became invalid.

Taking advantage of the break-up, Hitler started discussions with Mussolini. *El Duce,* finding the aggressive style of the Nazis more to his liking in 1936, told Hitler that he did not object to the rearmament of Germany and the annexation of Austria. Shortly thereafter, Hitler announced conscription and started to build up his army, navy, and air forces in direct defiance of the "Treaty of Versailles". Britain and France were too weak to prevent the rearmament and Mussolini, recognizing the strength of the Nazi movement, abandoned any attempt to side with the British and French, declaring his alliance with Germany.

The next step in the slippery slope to war was the Anschluss with Austria in 1938. Faced with the threat of invasion by Nazi Germany, the Austrian Chancellor resigned and allowed the German army to take power in Austria. This was welcomed by most Austrians as they shared a common ancestry with the German people. Britain and France did not have the strength to interfere, and could only watch the annexation of Austria with increasing concern.

As the German military forces built up in the ensuing months, the British government resigned themselves to being unable to turn back the steamroller advance of the Nazis. Hitler's attention then focused on the invasion of Poland. On September 30, 1938, Prime Minister Neville Chamberlain of Britain returned home from a meeting in Germany to declare "Peace for our time". This turned out to be an illusion, and Chamberlain was accused of appeasing Hitler. This was the point when the British government committed its powers to the preparation for war.

A year later, on September 1, 1939, German forces invaded Poland. Two days later, September 3, Britain declares war on Germany.

It was a lovely September day when we gathered in the

garden around the open window of the drawing room and listened to the stiff tones of Prime Minister Chamberlain on the radio declaring Britain was at war.

It meant little to me as a six-year-old, but I can imagine now that it must have been horrendous news to my parents. Especially to my father, who had already fought in the combat trenches in the First World War. In some ways, he may have thought he was fortunate because, of his seven children, the first three were all girls and unlikely to see action. The next four children were all boys with John, the eldest, only sixteen and, with the expectation that the war would be over by Christmas, his sons would not be required to fight. As it happened, it didn't turn out that way.

The declaration of war on the radio was followed by the national anthem and then the local air raid siren started up with its undulating, wailing message of warning. We would get to know that sound only too well over the next few years and each time we heard it, it would send a shiver of apprehension down our necks. It was followed by the monotone 'All Clear' siren which always created a sense of relief. As the war progressed, it was not unusual for the air raid alert to sound more than a few times a day.

Before going to school each morning, I would listen with hopeful anticipation for that familiar wail and with luck I might get a day off, as we were not required to catch the train to school if there was a raid on at the time we were due to leave home. During air raids, the trains would continue moving but at a reduced speed, presumably so that they had sufficient time to stop if the rails ahead were bombed. At school, we were required to take shelter during raids in one of the chambers in the crypt of the nearby Rochester Cathedral. If we were at home, we usually kept a watchful eye open for danger but kept on with normal activities.

As far as I was concerned, the new wartime condition had little effect on my life–if anything, it simply added a little more excitement to daily activities. Not so for my parents and all adults as it had been only two decades previously that WWI had ended. Memories were recalled of the terrible years of 1914 to 1918. The anxiety and stress of what was to come gripped the nation. This was partially offset by the quiet of the first few months which became known as the time of the "Phony War". This peaceful period was soon to be shattered with the defeat of the British Expeditionary Force at Dunkirk. This disaster changed the national psyche overnight and suddenly the prospect of a German invasion of Britain became a reality.

In the spring of 1940, with the improvement in the weather, the possibility of a German invasion became a real threat. Anti-invasion measures were undertaken everywhere. On the farm, wire cables were strung on posts everywhere there was flat land to foil the landing of German gliders, transporting soldiers. All sign posts on the roads were removed. Concrete gun emplacements, known as "pill boxes", appeared at strategic points on the roads. Part of the farm included flat marsh grazing land below sea level, behind the sea wall of the Thames estuary. A phony airstrip was marked out there complete with battery charged landing lights. If invading aircraft attempted to land there they would simply crash in the numerous large drainage ditches known as fleets.

My father buried fuel supplies, valuables, important paperwork and strategic pieces of equipment under the earthen floor in one of the two hop kilns on the farm. The mass evacuation of children from the cities to the countryside began. Extra supplies of food were stored away by citizens despite the national appeal to not hoard food. In summary, Britain prepared for the worst.

The invasion threat came to a crisis with the Battle of Britain in which the Royal Air Force fought for domination of the skies over Britain. This was the crucial battle: the prospect of invasion hung in its balance. By October 1940, the threat of invasion had lessened for the time being. It was not until Hitler decided to open up an eastern front against Russia that the imminent threat of invasion receded.

Brothers and Sisters

I was the youngest of seven children. By a stroke of good fortune, the three eldest were girls. The next four children were boys. The reason I say that we were fortunate is that the three eldest children, while of active service age, were not conscripted into the armed forces because they were female. However, this did not stop two of them signing on with the women's divisions. There are some interesting anecdotes to relate about my sisters but first ... the boys.

The eldest boy, John, was born in November 1924, which made him just sixteen when war was declared. For the first three years of the war, he was under age for the call up, and because he was working on the farm before the end of the war, he was excused active service altogether. He did however join the local Home Guard unit.

In the post-war years of the 50's, John French and his wife, Shelagh, were a major force in amateur steeplechase racing. With a stable of three or four thoroughbreds, they dominated the annual point-to-point racing over the jumps in south east England.

Shelagh also dominated the ladies' races on the point-to-point circuit, winning 59 races in the two-decade period of the 50's and 60's.

John is wishing Shelagh good luck in the ladies' race at the East Kent Hunt race meeting.

The second eldest son, Robert, while not conscripted, did see some action. At the age of thirteen, Robert joined the Royal Navy as a career. Instead of going to public school at the usual age, he committed himself to a life on the ocean waves, signing on at the Dartmouth Naval College. This set him on the path to service in the Royal Navy before the war ended. As a midshipman, fresh out of college, he served on HMS Viceroy, an old WWI destroyer built in 1917. They were on patrol in the North Sea when his ship sank a German U-boat off the coast of Scarborough. For this, he was decorated with the Distinguished Service Cross (DSC) at the tender age of nineteen. He continued his naval career throughout the war, seeing action in anti-submarine escort vessels mostly on the North Atlantic, and on the frigid Murmansk run.

There is an interesting anecdote from the U-boat sinking incident. When the wreckage of the submarine came to the surface, three cases containing 72 bottles of cognac were found strapped into one of the life rafts. Knowing that cognac was the favourite tipple of Sir Winston Churchill, the captain sent one of the cases to the Prime Minister. This may well have ensured the generous award of medals. There is no record of what happened to the other two cases, but the salvage laws of the sea are very generous to the victor and we can presume that very little cognac ever found its way ashore.

As for the third son in the family, Mick, like me, was too young to serve in the war. In 1945, he was seventeen and still at school. However, he was of a working age when he finished his studies and my father wasted no time including him in the running of the farm.

It may have been the Irish blood in his veins from the McClure family on his mother's side that prompted Mick's interest in horse racing. Or maybe it was the rivalry with his brother John's success on the race course that caused him to take up the same sport. This rivalry was consistent throughout their parallel farming careers.

John clearing the water jump in fine style on his favourite horse Magnesium Star.

The result was that Mick came home one day with Hymettus, a large and obstinate thoroughbred. His breeding was good as the famous Hyperion showed in the stud line of his forebears. He had the speed of a highly competitive race horse. The problem was his attitude. Hymettus could win just about any steeplechase he wanted to. The problem was that he didn't always want to.

In the very first steeplechase he entered with Mick in the saddle, he won by a quarter of a mile. Those punters who had taken the long odds with the bookmakers did very well. From that race forward, the bookies were never prepared to give him the long odds he really deserved.

It was anyone's guess as to what mood he was in when his name appeared on the race card. The first lap of the course was usually very encouraging. He would quickly open up a wide lead. All would go well until he realized that the other horses were not with him. He liked company, so he would simply stop until the others caught up. Only then would he proceed again at a pace that would keep his friends around him.

Not all his races were so frustrating as this photo attests. We knew he could win, and so he did in some major races, but the question was always which ones they would be!

John and Mick, continued to work the farm for the rest of their lives. If the cards had been dealt differently, and the sequence of birth had been the other way around with the four sons coming first, there might have been a very different story to tell. We were fortunate that no immediate family members were lost in WWII. The closest relative to have lost his life was a cousin named Fred Newcombe. He was a pilot in the Royal Air Force (R.A.F.). He failed to return from a mission, and is believed to have drowned in the North Sea. His body was never found. He had been married only a year or two and left behind a young widow and a daughter. They lived nearby in the village, and Betty, Fred's widow, was a good friend of my sisters.

With my three sisters being of an age that was expected to contribute to the war effort, it was interesting to see how each of them 'did their bit'. They had quite different personalities.

Mary was the eldest and, perhaps because she was the senior one, took on the responsible role of the steady and reliable matriarchal figure. When war broke out, she was twenty-one–a very significant age for a young lady. With six siblings all younger than her, she was saddled with the task of being my mother's helper. In fact, she virtually raised me at seventeen years old, when I was born. My sisters had little need for dolls; they had me as a plaything.

Mary's personality reflected the serious side of family responsibilities. It was fair to say that she was the steady one and she took her contribution to the family values very seriously. She did have one brief moment of independence. She had taken a course in cooking. Not the full-scale Cordon Bleu program, but one that taught her excellent baking and patisserie skills. Just before war was declared, she and her good friend, Betty Robertson, opened a tea shop in the nearby town of Gravesend. My father gave them a large sack of flour, a sack of sugar and £100 to get them started. I can just remember going to the little shop on Darnley Road and being treated to some of the best pastries I have ever tasted. As a six-year-old, I recall feeling very grown-up sitting at one of their little tables and being waited on like a real customer.

I believe their entrepreneurial undertaking would have done well if not for the war that came along and put an end to it. Mary returned to the family fold and helped at home. It wasn't long before she met Ronnie Maclean, a successful local farmer. From the start, she had made up her mind that he was the one for her and in 1940 they were married. It turned out to be a very successful marriage and Mary fulfilled the destiny of wife and mother for which she was so well suited.

My next eldest sister, Helen, faced a few rocky times when she was at school. Her health was not the best and she missed her schooling for the best part of a year. Eventually, she made an excellent recovery which is borne out by the fact that she has lived well into her nineties, longer than anyone else in the family.

Helen seemed to have a penchant for fliers. Just prior to WWII, she met a German air ace. He had made a name for himself by competing for Germany in the Schneider Trophy. This was an international air race held each year to establish the fastest single engine float plane over a triangular course of three landmarks. It was a popular event over a 340-km course which drew thousands of spectators. Since the trophy was won outright and retired by the British entry of a Supermarine Spitfire in 1931, his participation must have been before that year. The details are vague but, in the late 1930's, he met Helen and, on one occasion, flew her as a passenger in his plane to Paris. The relationship never developed, possibly due to the war or perhaps because the personal chemistry was not right. Interestingly, Helen later went on to marry another flier, but this time one on our own British side.

My sister Helen. Pictured here with Pepper, the family Fox Terrier.

With the outbreak of war, Helen signed up with the women's active services in the First Aid Nursing Yeomanry (FANY). This involved some nursing training, and basic mechanical skills for the maintenance of ambulances and other vehicles. After her training, she headed off in her army khakis to a small hospital in Moreton Hampstead in Devon. This was a hospital at which wounded service personnel were nursed back to health. Her primary duties involved driving ambulances carrying wounded servicemen.

Later, Helen's driving skills were also put to the test in the village as she was one of the volunteers who manned 'White Maria', the village ambulance. The white painted van with the big Red Cross signs on each side, and on the roof, was stationed in the yard at the farm. It saw duty on several occasions when called out for war casualties and civilian accidents. It was an old converted vehicle that had seen better days. It was always a question whether it would start when called out on an emergency but Helen's mechanical training in the FANY's was useful, and she was able to nurse it into life on most occasions.

The White Maria was garaged in the farm yard in a narrow shed with about eight inches to spare on each side: it required accurate parking. When parked for optimal driver access, there remained a gap of only two inches from the wall on the passenger side. This situation allowed just enough room for the driver to open her door and squeeze in behind the wheel. Fortunately, Helen was slim but it was difficult to back the vehicle out quickly in an emergency. It was equipped with a warning bell which had to be rung by the driver with one hand as she drove. Mercifully, there wasn't much traffic in the village, allowing driver and vehicle to provide timely emergency service on several occasions.

At some point in 1941, Helen met John Walliker, a Royal Air Force officer. As was often the case in wartime, the courtship was short-lived and they were married in 1942 in the local church, with a reception at the farm. To put on a lavish spread fit for the wedding, every food ration coupon that could be begged or borrowed from friends and neighbours was pooled together. The farm itself was a good source of some of the supplies and our flock of chickens was downsized for the occasion. A nice plump young lamb had an untimely accident behind the barn just a few days ahead of the big event. The lamb's unfortunate demise was probably attributed to enemy action. By any standards, the wedding feast was superb and I still recall the overstuffed feeling from eating too many cream cakes, dressed up in my tight-fitting Little Lord Fauntleroy suit with its starched collar.

Then there was my sister Pat. Younger than Helen by two years, Pat was just 18 when the war started. In many families, there has often been an ancestor of unusual character whose genes have reappeared in later generations. Pat fell into this category–her outgoing personality seemed in contrast with the rest of her steady and reliable siblings.

I have no idea if we had such an ancestor, but Pat had all indications of a throwback to a different set of genes. She was unusually tall for a girl in our family–at 5'7", she was three inches taller than her sisters and mother. Light-coloured hair is not unusual in our family but her hair was bright red. And she had the temperament to match. Wild is perhaps too strong a word to describe her personality; outgoing and adventurous are apt terms. There was a large dose of magnetism mixed with the rest of her traits that was borne out by the line-up of boys and men left in her slipstream. She had a strong personality that was bound to create an adventurous and up-and-down life. And so, it did.

Pat was always attracted to London and the social life it had to offer. Straight out of school, she took a secretarial course, opening the door to the city life which so attracted her. As soon as she had the qualifications and skills she needed, Pat headed for London at a time when most people were scrambling to leave the besieged capital to avoid the bombings. Although her real wish was to live in London so that she could savour the full delights of the cosmopolitan social life, she commuted daily by train. She obtained a secretarial position just as the real war started. Before long, she found a friend to share a flat and Pat achieved her goal of living mid-week in London, returning to the farm only at weekends.

For a while, the job went well but it was not to last. There was a change coming and it was probably something to do with the fact that many of her friends had quit the social life to go 'do their bit' for the war effort. So, Pat decided to follow suit. She made the decision to become a nurse. Anyone who knew Pat could have predicted that she was not cut out to be a nurse. After a few weeks of hard labour, insubordination with iron-willed matrons, and emptying bedpans, she realized she had made a mistake. But that was not a problem to Pat: one day, she simply handed in her bed pans and her nurse's uniform, and walked out the hospital door.

After a few days back on the farm, Pat decided that she could help the war effort best in the Women's Royal Naval Service, so she signed on to become a Wren. My sister looked good in the uniform. After all, the navy-blue outfit went well with her red hair. However, she didn't take too kindly to the square bashing required of all new recruits. Eventually, she got through and was assigned to a Fleet Air Arm base somewhere in the west of England. There was plenty of opportunity for a social life with the young men who were passing through the base learning how to fly and she was frequently invited to the parties in the officers' mess. The problem was that the young

Pat, in her official uniform, serving with the Women's Royal Naval Service. The Wrens.

men of her age were on the base for only a brief time before passing on to their active duty assignments. In the meantime, Pat spent her days wiping oil off the training aircraft and cleaning up after air sick flyers. As she described it, she got tired of bending over to clean up the insides of the cockpits only to have her bottom pinched by every passing air crew member.

Pat needed more out of life than this routine. The glamour of being a Wren was beginning to wear off. The status quo was not enough--she needed excitement and a better social life. The red-headed personality was about to take charge once again. After a particularly boring period of dull routine and bottom pinching, Pat had had enough. She changed back into civvies and, leaving her uniform on her bunk, she once again walked out the gate. My sister became a deserter from His Majesty's forces.

Apparently, the regulations governing the desertion of men in uniform did not apply to women. For a man, it was a serious offence; for women, it was of lesser consequence and there were no repercussions. Pat turned up back at the farm and set about re-organizing her life. It was now 1943 and the tides of war had changed. The Americans had signed on, bringing with them an air of optimism to the Allied war effort. The raids on London were now restricted to night time and, with the arrival of the US forces, London social life had regained some of its pre-war glamour.

Once again Pat was drawn to the bright lights of the city, like a moth to a candle. She decided that she had to live there full time to better enjoy the lively social scene. Her secretarial skills were still intact and in great demand in London. Suitable accommodation was in short supply as the housing supply had been hit severely by all the bombing. No new residential housing had been built so finding a suitable flat to rent was not easy. Pat still had plenty of friends in town and she soon found a flat mate to share with her, but they had to accept what accommodation was available on their limited salaries.

It wasn't until I was taken to her flat that I realized how difficult it was to find safe accommodation. I don't recall which part of London she lived in but it was showing the results of the frequent bombing. Pat could only afford a modest rent, so her options were few. When we arrived on the street where she lived, several of the houses were no more than a pile of rubble. Her building was one of the few ones remaining upright and it stayed that way thanks to some heavy timbers supporting the one side where another house had been but was now a heap of rubble. It was a four-storey walk-up and Pat's flat was on the top floor. As Pat said, "I have a nice panoramic view of London thanks to Adolf". Clearly, she felt the risk of a long drop from the top floor courtesy of another bomb was worth the pay-off for a good view and proximity to the social life of the city.

It was a fascinating time to be single and attractive in London. Pat was never the shy and retiring type, so it was not long before she was mixing with the attractive young men from all the different countries making up the Allied Forces. It was on one of those social occasions when she met Gilmore Bell, a handsome and impressive fighter pilot from South Africa. He was flying with the R.A.F. and, like most adventurous young men, spent as much leave time as possible in London. Evidently, they hit it off right away and, following the wartime custom, became engaged after a short courtship. The engagement was probably hastened along by the R.A.F., who posted Gilmore to help in the invasion of Italy in 1943. It seemed a quick engagement was the natural thing to do with all the uncertainties of life in war time.

With Gilmore away, life had now changed for Pat. It was not so much fun hitting the hot spots of the London social scene as an engaged woman of 22. It cramped her style considerably. Now, as her previous careers had illustrated, Pat was not one to accept the situation when there were other options available. As the Allies fought their way up the boot of Italy, Gilmore was moved north to airbases just behind the front lines. Communication with front line troops was difficult, especially if you wanted to know where they were. I have no idea how Pat found out where Gilmore was stationed, but somehow, she pulled enough strings to find out that he was in Vittorio Veneto in the province of Treviso in northern Italy.

Finding out his location was one thing, but that was not enough for Pat. Tired of being the lonely fiancée for even a short time, she set about to be with him. No account of this will appear in any war records yet, in the spring of 1944, Pat finagled a ride to the front lines in Italy though the fighting was still in full swing. We don't know if Gilmore was in on the plan, but, when she just turned up at his forward base in Vittorio, he professed complete surprise. It didn't take long for the base commander to authorize a wedding ceremony and a big party at the base ensued.

How long Pat remained in Italy is not clear, but it seems likely that she was hustled back to Britain without much delay. Of course, she now returned as a married woman. She returned to her job in London until her husband was de-mobbed in 1945. In short order, Gilmore packed up and took his bride back to South Africa. Four children followed quickly and Gilmore, ever the optimist, struggled unsuccessfully to find a steady career. The strain became too much for Pat trying to raise a family of four; after ten years or so, she and the children returned to the UK and back to the farm. Divorce followed.

But there is more to this story: Pat married again a year or two later. By chance, she met another man, Peter Bell. Despite having the same last name, he was not related to the first Mr. Bell. Peter was an industrial designer, who worked on such projects as the layout of the cockpit for the Concorde supersonic plane. He was also an avid collector of antique glassware and other items from the 17th and 18th century. After the wedding, Pat did not have to change her married name.

They had a child, Pat's fifth offspring. The new husband was an interesting and reliable fellow but unable to provide the excitement Pat craved. The marriage did not work out and they were divorced after a year or two.

The climax to this saga occurred about 25 years after Pat's first marriage, when her eldest daughter was about to be married. The first Mr. Bell, Gilmore, walked his daughter down the aisle of the church and walked back up the aisle with Pat on his arm. Pat stayed on his arm and they lived happily together again as man and wife until Gilmore died many years later. They never bothered to get re-married. There was no need–she was, and always had been, Mrs. Pat Bell.

Pat blazed a trail through life. With her red hair and the temperament to go with it, she provided colour and glamour at a time when life needed brightening up. Maybe this was Pat's most important contribution to the war effort.

My six siblings and I, posing for a portrait. Guess which one I am. I have always been fond of dogs...

Gas Masks

As early as July 1939 everyone in Britain was issued with a gas mask. The experience of the fatal injuries caused by mustard and other gases in the First World War led our politicians to expect the worst. Poison gas had also been used at Guernica in the Spanish Civil War in 1938. There was every reason to believe that the Nazis would use gas again in WWII. In July of 1939 the government issued gas masks to all citizens with the proviso that the possibility of war existed and the masks would likely be necessary.

These contraptions that made everyone look like visitors from outer space were supplied in two or three sizes and even special ones were provided for babies in their cribs. We all had to be fitted with them and once war was declared we were required to carry them with us at all times. If you look at wartime photos you will often see people with little square boxes suspended on a string hung over their shoulders. In photos of children on the London train platforms being evacuated out of the big cities every one of them had that little square box slung over one shoulder and a luggage label with their name on it tied to their lapels. It was probable that few of those poorly constructed gas masks survived the tearing, fighting, and confusion of the train journey to the safe havens that weeping parents saying goodbye wished for their children.

The gas masks were crude devices manufactured in a hurry and in vast quantities. The main part which fitted over the top of the head and tightly round the face was made of rubber. They provided limited vision through the Bakelite eye goggles. The round filter device in the front would quickly dry out if left exposed for any long length of time, and therefore become ineffective. Wearing one was a claustrophobic experience and led to much laughter as we looked as though we had a trunk like an elephant. To alleviate the fears of the children the masks were referred to as their Mickey Mouse faces.

Fortunately, we never had to use them for anything other than practice but it was just as well because the constant carrying of them in their flimsy cardboard boxes led to early cracks in the rubber and face pieces. I know that my gas mask developed a crack in the face piece within the first three months. My mother simply said, 'here take mine' and didn't worry that her mask would no longer keep out any gas. After a year or so we all relaxed about the dangers of a gas attack and although we still had to have them with us when out of the home no one seemed to care that they were falling apart. As the threat of a gas attack seemed to lessen over time fewer people bothered to carry the masks with them.

Steel Overhead

It was a matter of pride among boys of my age, to recognize every type of plane that flew in the skies above us. The aircraft identification posters issued by the government were much sought after by collectors and information gatherers such as myself. Along with posters urging us to "waste not, want not" and "keep calm and carry on" or reminding us that "loose lips sink ships", these aircraft identification posters could be found in public places such as near air raid shelters, on station platforms and anywhere the public could see them.

I had a particular advantage in that I lived on the farm in open country on a small rise in the land. I could look out of my bedroom window and enjoy a panoramic view of the landscape towards the River Thames estuary. The German pilots often used the bird's-eye view of the river as a road map to London and thus provided an excellent opportunity for identifying the type of aircraft in the sky.

In the early months of the war, the German bombers flew in daylight hours and could be seen readily with the naked eye. From my upland viewpoint there were times when low-flying bomber formations seemed to be flying at a height parallel to my location. This provided the opportunity to match my angle of viewing with the side view illustrations on the identification posters. For instance, the Heinkel HE 111 bombers were easily identified by the "glasshouse" structure of the cockpit area. Admittedly at a great distance, but we used to kid ourselves we could see the aircrew inside.

My friends and I could soon identify all the bomber types that flew overhead. We could tell the difference between the fast light-bomber Dorniers, known as "flying pencils" due to their slim shape, the heavier Junkers 88 and the Heinkel HE 111s. The German fighters were harder to identify because of their smaller size and faster speed, but with a clear view we could spot a Messerschmitt109 and the less frequently seen Focke-Wulf 190.

The sound of the aircraft engines was also distinctive. The heavy grinding sound of a squadron of bombers on its way to London, fully loaded with bombs, was very different from the return journey of the survivors as they returned. The screaming efforts of a wounded aircraft headed home was reminiscent of the scream of a terrified rabbit in the jaws of a fox.

Later in the war, the population of Britain learned to identify the sound of the jet engine of the V1 flying bombs in safe overhead flight. As soon as that sound spluttered and stopped it was time to hit the nearest ditch as it would be followed a few moments later with an explosion as it crashed when its jet fuel burned out.

As the war progressed and the balance switched in favour of the Allies, the opportunity to spot identities was diminished as the German bombers were limited to night raids.

It is reassuring to have a quarter inch of steel overhead when the bombs start to fall. In 1941, a lorry drew into the yard at home; the rear end was dropped exposing a pile of steel and packages of bolts. My father and brothers gathered round to help the driver remove his heavy delivery. The small stuff came first; about 200 steel bolts and nuts. This was followed by long angle irons. Some welded steel mesh panels, which were a little lighter, followed but the final item was a flat steel sheet measuring 6 feet 6 inches by 4 feet. It took four men to carry this into the centre room of the house. This was to be my bed for the next two years. It was a Morrison shelter.

Our farmhouse was three hundred years old. At various times additions had been made to the original cottage in the centre of the house. This centre room had a beamed ceiling of fifteen inch square oak beams. You could still recognize the shape of the first growth trees in the roughly finished logs. English oak is the wood that was used to construct Henry the Eighth's men-of-war ships. It is the strongest wood native to England. As the additions to the house grew out from this central cottage, five doors had been added to access these newer rooms.

A direct hit on any house was likely to collapse the whole structure regardless of how well it was built. In the more likely event of a near miss, the danger came from the possible collapse of one or more walls, thus bringing down the ceiling. There was no doubt the ceiling could take the weight of the second and third floors of the house but not if the supporting walls were knocked down. A falling ceiling then became the hand of death itself for anyone underneath it. Our oak beams seemed to offer reassurance but the real facts were different: government research revealed this danger and had developed the Morrison shelter to reduce the casualties from collapsing houses. My parents decided it was the prudent thing to construct this steel shelter-cum-table in this central room.

It took a long time to figure out the brief instructions on how to put it all together. This could be forgiven as there had not been much time to produce these shelters since war was declared. Over 400,000 were hastily manufactured and distributed in 1940 and another 100,000 in 1944 with the threat from Hitler's V1 flying bombs. The kit consisted of a total of 350 pieces and came with three tools to use in its construction. With so many pieces to assemble it was two or three hours before we could put the kettle on and view the finished work over a cup of tea. To say it was solid would be an understatement. It was a massive intrusion into the room. Its presence demanded that it would become the family focal point for most household activities. We still used the dining room when there were too many to fit around the steel table but for everyday use it was fine. The only thing you had to be careful about was that you didn't catch your knee or some other part on its square edges. A few swear words at dinner time were understood and accepted.

Being six feet six inches by four feet, it provided enough space for three people to sleep under. But with four occupants, it was a tight fit unless some were children. In an extreme emergency one or two more could squeeze in for shelter but not for sleeping. At ground level, metal slats were woven across each other to provide a crude form of springs. With a mattress on top of that it was reasonably comfortable for a ten-year-old; for adults, it was downright miserable. On three sides of the table,

The Morrison Shelter. Safe in an air raid, but not the most comfortable sleeping accommodation!

welded wire grids protected the sleepers from any debris that might come in from the sides.

As a family, we used the table for sleeping on a regular basis for the first few months and during the worst of the raids in 1940 and 1941. The one hold-out was my father, who refused to leave his big feather bed upstairs for any reason. He had survived the Germans in WWI and was damned if he was going to let them intimidate him this time around. The close proximity of three or four bodies in such a small space was not conducive to a good night's sleep. One by one family members abandoned the safety of the table for a good sleep in their own beds elsewhere. As the air raids became less frequent in the later stages of the war, we all opted for comfort at the expense of safety. But still the Morrison shelter dominated the house. It was the elephant in the room that dictated our household arrangements. I was not permitted to return to my bedroom upstairs so a safe place on the ground floor was allocated to me. My bedroom became a narrow passageway between the centre room and what we called the nursery. It was on the ground floor and well protected with overhead beams and had no outside wall exposure so it was relatively safe. There was no longer any need for a nursery so the room at the end of the six-foot passage had become the farm office. I was quite comfortable on the floor in the passage on a mattress except that anyone going into the office had to step over me. There was little opportunity for me to sleep in without having my older brothers' feet passing within inches of my tender body parts. As you can imagine, I got little sympathy from my brothers if I tried to have a lie-in and some of those footsteps were carelessly misplaced on purpose.

The dangers of a collapsing ceiling were easily understood, but even under the protection of the steel table there was always the risk of flying glass shards if a bomb blast shattered the windows. Glass fragments would whiz horizontally across the room in the event of a near miss. To alleviate some of this risk, we stuck special air raid tape in big X's on each window pane. The sticky tape was designed to help hold broken pieces of glass together if the window shattered.

After dark, the danger from flying glass pieces was further reduced by the blackout curtains on the inside of all windows. To ensure that all homes followed the blackout regulations, the village air raid wardens would pedal their bikes around after dark to look for houses with light showing from rooms where someone had forgotten to draw the blackout blinds or even chinks of light showing through improperly drawn blinds. I liked to think they were looking for German spies signalling to overhead aircraft but it was easy for innocent folks to forget to draw all the blinds securely. On more than one occasion there was a knock on our front door and a cry of "put that light out".

In warmer weather the safest thing to do at night was to open the windows in every room where someone was sleeping. In the event of a bomb falling nearby, the blast would simply pass through the open window without breaking the glass. We could do this in an older house such as ours as the windows were mostly of the hinged type which could be opened outwards. It was better to accept the cooler temperatures in favour of better security. We could always throw on another blanket. On one such an occasion a bomb fell in the nearby meadow and the blast came through the open windows as we lay under the Morrison shelter. The blackout curtains swung into the room and up to the ceiling. The blast flew over us, went down the front hall and somehow rattled the front door so that it opened inward. From there it passed out through the door. It had passed harmlessly through the house from one end to the other. How it opened the front door inwardly remains a mystery. We were just thankful that it had made a brief visit and then moved on. Bomb blasts were unpredictable.

The Morrison shelter was suitable for our house as we had the space to accommodate it. Where there was insufficient space inside the home, households were offered an outside shelter designed to fit into even the smallest of gardens. It was known as the Anderson shelter. Three million of these structures were distributed by the government. For the poor, they were made available free; anyone earning more than five pounds per week could purchase the kit for seven pounds. The Anderson shelters were set two feet into the ground and consisted of straight sheets galvanized corrugated panels for the sides and overhead shaped panels bolted together forming a curved roof six feet high. Each end had a steel wall with the entrance at one end protected by an earthen blast wall. The whole structure was designed to be further protected by a foot or two of earth over the whole shelter. Bunks inside were designed to sleep six people.

Although tests showed that these shelters were highly protective, the population did not like using them. With the floor two feet below ground level they were subject to flooding or at least a wet and dank atmosphere. Second, it was necessary to leave the house in order to enter the shelter in the garden. Their use was particularly unpopular at night as the shelter was lit only by whatever the owner brought with him and the lighting was subject to the strict blackout regulations. Many of these structures went unused throughout the war however they were put to good use as garden sheds and storage shelters in peace time. Half a century after the war, a friend of mine used his shelter for growing a fine crop of mushrooms thanks to the damp and dark interior. If you take a train ride through the London suburbs you can often look down into the postage stamp-sized back gardens of the row houses to see, nearly seventy-five years after WWII, some relics of the Anderson shelters still in use.

Much publicity has been given to the use of the London Underground stations as public shelters. Whole families virtually lived there, at least during the night hours. Squatters' rights were fiercely defended to hold the most favoured places. I remember seeing the heaps of household items piled on the platforms as I travelled on the Underground trains on those rare occasions when I was taken up to London.

Many of the stations were deep underground and would not be affected by bombing on the surface. It is interesting to note that the government initially banned their use as shelters. The reasons stated for this were that they were unsanitary and could spread disease especially as few were fitted with toilets and that in the event of a panic, someone would slip on the stairs and the crush of people entering the Tube stations would cause a catastrophe. Sadly, on at least one occasion, the government was right about this latter point.

Taking refuge from the Air Raids in a London Tube Station.

On the night of September 7, 1940, the London Blitz started with wave after wave of bombers targeting the London docks in the east end of town. As the blitz continued and thousands were killed, people took matters into their own hands. On September 19, the crowds fleeing the bombing simply descended into the stations with bedding and food supplies. The station managers accepted the situation and assisted the terrified residents as best they could. Two days later, the government reversed its decision, opening the station platforms as public shelters, appointing shelter supervisors and supplying toilet facilities, health workers and canteens. By five o'clock each day, Londoners were streaming into the Tube stations, taking bedding and other supplies with them. There was a rush to stake claims to the best places on the platforms even as the evening rush hour of trains and commuters were passing through the stations. A short section of the Piccadilly Line was closed to trains, the power was cut off, and the rail lines concreted over. This section of the Underground became a permanent air raid shelter.

A total of 170,000 Londoners used the Underground system for shelter during the worst of the bombing. Not all their experiences were favourable and there was some loss of life from direct hits. In one case, at the Balham station, a bomb burst a water main and 68 people died. The worst loss of life occurred at the Bethnal Green station where 173 people were crushed when someone slipped on the stairs as a crowd of 1,500 rushed to take shelter. The panic was caused by the loud bang of a new type of anti-aircraft rocket fired nearby that the people mistook for a falling bomb.

Meanwhile my family continued our fitful sleep under the steel table. There was even some comfort in hearing the heavy snoring coming from upstairs as my father showed his disdain for the German efforts to intimidate us. Over time, we became inured to the sounds and risks of the frequent raids.

Taking Cover

Taking shelter in air raids usually resulted in a battle of wills between my mother, or other family members, and me. My shrapnel collection was the primary interest in my life and it was important to hear and locate where interesting bits fell out of the sky during the raids. The best place to spot the descent of these treasures was at the back door to the kitchen. I liked to stand in the open door and would duck back in the doorway when the scream of a falling bomb or the whistle of exploded anti-aircraft shells were a bit too close for comfort

Often it would take the severe chastisement of my father to get me back inside the house. In reality, it was a case of the pot calling the kettle black, as my father liked to do the same as I did and used his authority to usurp my prime observation point. In his mind, he was less interested in collecting the bits and pieces from above and more interested in noting where damage to the roofs of the farm buildings might occur. What was worse than roof damage was the possibility of fires resulting from high explosive or incendiary bombs falling on the farm buildings. This was a particular concern if livestock was sheltered inside.

The possibility of injury from both enemy and friendly action was very real. There was one occasion when I ventured out too soon after some German planes had passed overhead and marked where a juicy bit of shrapnel fell. I had noted that something had hit the roof of one of the stables. It had broken some roofing slates and the piece of whatever it was had either slid to the ground or penetrated the stable roof. It might have been the nose cone of an anti-aircraft shell, in which case it was a collector's item if it was still in one piece. I waited impatiently as I allowed what I thought would be sufficient time for all of the falling bits and pieces to land. Having marked the probable location of my prospective treasure, I abandoned the safety of the kitchen doorway and rushed out to search for the next piece to add to my collection.

Sure enough, there it was and indeed it was a nose cone, a valuable treasure that could be swapped at school for another piece of shrapnel which would add to the uniqueness of my collection. As I bent down to retrieve the harvest of the sky, there was a little sizzle followed by a *chink* as a final piece of exploded shell landed at my feet. No harm was done except for a small gouge in the asphalt but it did shake me up to realize the very real danger of being too hasty in emerging from the safety of cover. The offending piece was added to my collection but a small, jagged piece of metal of no obvious ancestry was of little value on the trading floor at school.

My father was a hero of World War One, having received the Military Cross for capturing twelve German soldiers while on night patrol between the two opposing trench lines in France. He had received a flesh wound in this action but had recovered well. For several of my gullible, young years he had fooled me with his comments when he couldn't keep up with my much faster running or fooling around. His excuse would be "I've got a bone in my leg, you know". As a lad, I attributed this to his war wound.

My father survived the First World War and very nearly emerged unscathed in the Second. However, his wounds in the latter conflict were more to his pride and dignity than to his body. One night he had taken over my favourite lookout post by the back door. This air raid was a particularly noisy one and he was keen to spot any damage to the house or farm buildings. The rest of my family was safely inside the house when we heard the loud scream of something large descending. Later we discovered it was an unexploded anti-aircraft shell that buried itself in the meadow behind the house. It was close enough to give us all concern but instead of hearing the expected explosion, the sudden silence following its arrival was broken by a loud clattering of something metal--and then a thump. This was quickly followed by a lot of swearing and more clanking. After a short pause my father entered the kitchen bleeding from a head wound. At first, we thought he was the victim of enemy action, but then we glanced down to see he had one foot firmly wedged in a metal bucket with grey ash clinging to his pant leg. After we had extracted his foot from the bucket and my mother cleaned up the blood running down his face, he explained the mystery.

The house was heated mostly by wood fires in the rooms we usually occupied. Each day it was a chore to clean out the ash from the fire grates. Since wood ashes are very light, they have a tendency to fly around the house. To avoid the ash dust in the house as quickly as possible the ash bucket was put outside the kitchen door for later spreading as fertilizer on the garden.

At the sound of a possible bomb coming down so close to the house, my father quickly stepped back to take shelter. His hurried step backward in the dark resulted in his foot entering the ash bucket and his shoe becoming securely jammed inside. With no time to spare he tried to take another step with his foot in the bucket only to trip over and hit his head on the side of a cement drain. With the greater peril judged to be the falling bomb or other projectile, he continued his bucket-footed progress into the house where he was greeted with laughter by his unsympathetic family members.

The head wound was washed and bandaged and the bucket removed from his foot. When the emergency medical procedures had been completed, we all stood back and broke out the beer to celebrate the survival of our war hero. Then he was packed off to bed by my mother.

There was always a tense half hour or so after each air raid when we hoped the telephone would not ring. If it did ring, it was likely to tell us of some damage that had been observed somewhere on the farm. A few tiles off the roof of a barn or a broken window were not considered worth bothering with at night. Basic repairs, if needed, could be carried out later. What we did fear was the damage from exploded bombs or, worse still, the myriad small fires caused by incendiary bombs. These bombs, weighing perhaps two pounds each, were engineered to land and ignite with just a small explosion. Packed with some kind of magnesium compound that would fizzle and burn for a few minutes. They were designed to set fire to any combustible material within a radius of about four feet.

Individual incendiary bombs were not a problem to handle; as they could be safely approached and smothered with dirt or other non-combustible material. On the other hand, if you attempted to put them out with water, it was important to soak the burning fuel thoroughly. If the chemicals are not thoroughly soaked, they can easily break out into flames again. In an open area, each bomb could be neutralized simply with a shovel. If the fire spread before the bomb had been found, it was a more serious matter.

Incendiary bombs were dropped in what were known as "bread baskets". These were metal drum-type canisters that would open during their descent from the bomber and scatter the small bombs over a wide area of a hundred yards or more. It was not unusual to come across the battered remains of these breadbaskets lying harmlessly on the ground after an incendiary raid.

Fortunately, incendiary bombs were unreliable and many would fail to ignite upon hitting the ground. It was not unusual to find ten or twenty unexploded bombs scattered about a field with perhaps another ten small burn circles where others had ignited but did little more than create a patch of burned turf. Since we knew the unexploded ones were relatively harmless if handled carefully, we would simply pick them up and pile them against the trunk of a nearby tree until such time as the authorities could get around to collecting them for disposal. This would sometimes take weeks.

The Air Raid Wardens in the village would make a point of watching for falling bombs during a raid. When any were spotted as having fallen on my father's property, we would receive the dreaded phone call. One of the farm cars was equipped with basic firefighting equipment such as shovels, sand bags and buckets. When the call came, my father, brothers and I would drive to where the bombs were thought to have landed. Often there was not much we could do as there would simply be a big crater where a high explosive bomb had landed. If this was in a field, we would just check that no livestock were affected either through downed fences or perhaps injury, and then return home. If there was a fire then it was another matter altogether; we would attempt to put it out usually with the help of the village fire brigade volunteers.

By the war's end, the countryside was pockmarked with bomb craters in the open fields, and many of the farm and residential buildings were in a shabby state. We were fortunate when compared to the city of London and other cities in the south of England.

The Drop In

His boots hit the ground first. As he rolled to break the impact, the symbol of the Luftwaffe, the silver eagle, flashed briefly into view. As he sat up the parachute settled gently about his shoulders like a shroud.

But this was not the end for the German pilot. Even in war there are times when humanity transcends the brutality of the conflict. This was a gentleman warrior who may have been captured, but not defeated.

This is the story of the German prisoner of war I helped to capture. I was nine years old at the time. I was standing in awe in an open field while fifty planes engaged in mortal combat overhead. This was at the height of the Battle of Britain. On a clear day, the sky became a canvas of intertwining contrails as the fighter planes wove in and out in their deadly dance. At times the sky was a scene of unraveling and knotted trails of condensation among the cotton wool clouds of a perfect summer afternoon.

The newly formed lines in the sky at first were tight and well defined. Over the course of a minute or two, the edges became ragged and the clear delineation started to fade as the wind scattered the white puffy tracks. Interspersed with these positive white lines was the occasional black vertical line of smoke from a wounded aircraft. Such lines would always be descending, sometimes straight to earth, sometimes in a spiral of death throes, and sometimes in a curve, as the pilot fought at the controls to bring his steed to a softer landing … always downward and always with the colour of death.

Of course, we would stand there and cheer on the Spitfires and the Hurricanes as they duelled with the enemy's Messerschmitts and Dorniers. It was all there right before our eyes as though it was a performance specially staged for us bystanders. We watched for an attacking plane to get into a commanding position and then waited for the rat-a-tat-tat of its cannons. A hit was unmistakeable. First, we would see a flame and then oily smoke would be the tell-tale of the knockout punch. While we would be cheering on our own team, we would switch to neutrality as a plane began its death fall from the sky. At this point all bias was abandoned and the watching crowd started to root for the pilot regardless of nationality.

"Bail out, bail out!" we cried as all who beheld this final act projected and prayed in support of humanity, regardless of the uniform. One…two… three seconds passed as we imagined the pilot struggling with his canopy. As the seconds ticked by, we would fear for his life and the impending fate that awaited his abrupt return to earth. Five… six… seven … "there he is, he's out just in time!" the crowd shouted as we saw the sudden white bloom of the flower that was his parachute and ticket to life.

In one such instance, those of us working at harvest time in the stubble of the wheat fields had the opportunity to play more than just a bystander's role in this theatre of the sky. As a nine-year-old, I was paid sixpence an hour to do my small part in bringing in the summer's harvest. Labour was always in short supply as the regular able-bodied workers were conscripted into the armed services. Those that were left were the young, the elderly and anyone else who could turn out to 'do their bit', as the wartime saying went. Not the least of these helpers were the ladies of The Women's Land Army. This was an organization for those women who preferred to work on farms rather than in the munitions factories. Usually there was a half dozen or so of these well-muscled ladies billeted in the village to work on local farms.

It was a warm August day and yet another of those occasions during the Battle of Britain when the skies were filled with combat. We had paused in our daily routine of 'stooking' the sheaves of wheat in rows so that the grain would dry out over the next two or three days. All eyes were on the battle unfolding above us when we noticed a German Messerschmitt had been knocked out of the sky. We counted down the seconds and with much relief we saw that the pilot had successfully bailed out. His parachute opened and he began the descent. It was a southerly wind and although his plane was seen to crash a mile or more away from us to the south, it was apparent that he was coming ever closer. At first there was just a feeling of relief that he would be safe but, as he descended, we noticed that he was coming our way. He was getting nearer...lower...and likely to land quite close by.

Fascination with the spectacle turned to nervousness and, finally, to near panic. What were we expected to do? Should we run for our lives or should we stand our ground and take on this enemy combatant face to face. Quickly, I was bundled out of danger to the rear of our army of harvest warriors. Our hesitation decided the role for us to play. As the pilot descended, the brave team of elderly farm workers, Land Army ladies, assorted children and dogs grabbed their pitch forks or any item that would boost their courage.

Our unexpected visitor came to a gentle grounding in our midst. There was a long silence during which our weapons trembled and our courage wavered. The fighter pilot rose to his feet and carefully gathered up his parachute. Still not a word was spoken as we wondered what to do next. The spell was broken by our prisoner, or was it that we were his prisoners?

"Good afternoon ladies and gentlemen," said the tall, smartly uniformed young man in perfect English. "I wonder if any of you could offer me a light?" said this elegant creature from space as he drew out a silver cigarette case from his pocket.

"That was a rather harrowing experience but I do apologize for dropping in on you like this." This unexpected turn of events was enough to break the tension and a nervous laugh went up from us, his captors. Now we knew for sure who was captured and who were the captors. The proper balance had been restored.

"I suppose you should relieve me of this" said the prisoner, as he tossed his pistol on the ground. At this, one of our numbers stepped forward and lit the man's cigarette and the wavering pitch forks were lowered. The pistol stayed where it had landed.

It was just a matter of a few minutes until we heard the tinkling of a bicycle bell and George, the village policeman, arrived. Authority was at hand and we had all 'done our bit' for the war effort. The two adversaries marched off side-by-side to the waiting Home Guard lorry that had driven across the stubble to collect our gentleman prisoner.

The battle in the sky was over and the crisscross of those contrails had begun to fade as the wind washed away the scars of war. The farm lunch wagon arrived with my mother at the wheel accompanied by one of my sisters. It was the daily routine when they brought the giant teapot that served a dozen thirsty people. Work never did quite resume that afternoon. The adrenaline subsided and was replaced with a sense of pride for a job well done. The sheaves of wheat could wait for one more day. Arrangements were made to meet at the "Fox and Hounds" pub that night to take full advantage of the heroism that had been displayed and to feign reluctance in accepting the free beers which could rightly be expected. This had been a day to be savoured, to be ruminated upon and tucked away in the memory to be trotted out in later years for our future grandchildren.

I returned home with a chest bursting with pride and knowing that I, too, had played my part, however small, in the war effort.

WWII was one step nearer victory for the good guys.

Evacuation

In the years between 1939 and 1950, I was a student at three schools but in five different locations. The five locations were the result of the wholesale removal of two of the schools because of the demands of war. The safety of school children was a top priority but the need to win the war was a factor too.

My first school was St. Michaels Preparatory School in Uckfield, Sussex. Since it was just south of London, it was considered to be in a dangerous area. As a result, all the pupils and most of the staff were evacuated to a safer location in Devon in the south west of England away from threat of bombing.

I was never really happy at St. Michaels, possibly because I was away from home at a very young age during the stress-filled war years. My parents no doubt thought it would be best for me to be away from the bombing in Kent. I can understand their thinking but separation from family during these anxious times resulted in my unhappiness at St. Michaels.

The second boarding school I attended was Malvern College in Worcestershire. The buildings and grounds were expropriated in 1939 by the government for the development of the British radar system. "Out you go--we need all your facilities" was the order. "Our research is top secret, so don't tell a soul" came the no-appeal instructions.

So, Malvern College packed up what they could take in a hurry and scrambled to find premises elsewhere to keep the school going. The first move was to Blenheim Palace, the home of the Duke of Marlborough, Winston Churchill's ancestor.

I recall visiting my older brother there. One hundred or more beds were set up in the great hall. The improvised sport, thought up by the students, was to see who could throw their rolled socks up toward the very high ceiling, catching them in the filigree stone carvings that illuminated the high surface. On glancing up I saw socks of all colours suspended above us. The ceiling was so high I have no idea how the staff could get them down unless the socks stretched out and fell of their own accord.

That was only the first move for Malvern College. After a year or so at Blenheim Palace, an offer of accommodation came from Harrow School at Harrow-On-The-Hill, just west of London. With the demands of the war for active duty personnel, I suspect that pupil enrollment had dropped at this famous school and some facilities were underused. Certainly, the set-up was more appropriate than the large draughty rooms of the palace so the offer to move was accepted. It was at this point in 1946 when I became a new boy there as a 13-year-old.

Winston Churchill was Harrow School's most celebrated alumnus and, with his family connection to Blenheim Palace, I have often wondered if he orchestrated these two moves on behalf of Malvern College. A word from Winston may have been all it took to arrange these matters. It is pleasant to speculate that Churchill took time off from his more pressing engagement with the war to help out.

In 1947, the home grounds at Malvern in Worcestershire were handed back to the school and it was this return to the school's home base that found me yet again on the move.

But back to the beginning of my schooling. It was the custom in pre-war days for parents at a certain income level to send their children to boarding school. This was the case in my family and somehow, despite relatively modest means, all seven children were educated for most of their school years away from home. In my case, I was bundled off to boarding school at St. Michaels following in the footsteps of my three brothers. I was only six years' old and the youngest boy at the school. This may sound like harsh and uncaring treatment by my parents but there were two reasons why they may have made this decision. My father had fought in the trenches during WWI and had no illusions about the horrors of war. In 1939, before war was declared, there was much speculation that it was inevitable. Knowing that our home was in the flight path for German bombers and possibly invasion troops, it would be safer for me to be away from the worst of the action. Uckfield was also in the line of fire but preparations had been made to move the school to a safer location if war was declared. Knowing this, I believe my parents felt that I would be safer away from home. Another factor was that one of my older brothers, Mick, was already at the school. At five years my senior, he could keep a protective eye on his six-year-old sibling. Well, that was the theory anyway. In practice, we both went our own separate ways!

Dropped off at school for the first time in the May of 1939, I was not a happy camper. But then all of the other dozen or so new boys were in the same state. For the first few nights, quiet sobs came from most of the beds in my new dormitory. However, it was not long before the routines of the school absorbed us and our new-found world became tolerable. Our studies were not demanding and the atmosphere was friendly. I particularly enjoyed the daily sports in the afternoon. Cricket became an obsession and I can still recall the tiny cricket bat I was given that was supposedly the right size for a six-year-old. The wickets were the same size as for the adult game and were, therefore, about ten inches wide. I put up a valiant effort in defending my wicket with my three-inch-wide bat but to little avail. Eventually the teachers took pity on me and substituted a bat with twice the width. I struggled with the weight of my new weapon but was able to stay batting at the wicket for a few more balls instead of retreating in tears after being consistently bowled out with the first ball.

Just as I was getting accustomed to my new friends and the school routines, we were all sent home for two weeks while the whole school was packed up and moved to its new home at Tawstock Court near Barnstaple in North Devon. Since the bombing and the Battle of Britain had started, my mother and I went to stay with some farming friends, the Rimells, in Hampshire. Their son was also a pupil at St. Michaels. It was considered a safe haven where the bombing risks were less than in our home county of Kent.

I remember this brief period well as the weather was hot and sunny, and the farmhouse and its setting were right out of a picture book. Nearby was the River Test, a well renowned trout river revered by fly fishermen. For us, it was the perfect location for our frequent picnics on its banks. In the hot weather, we had many enjoyable swims in its cool and clear waters. It was an interlude of bucolic peace well away from the tumult of the war in the rest of the country. Our peaceful pleasures faced no more interruption than the game of hide and seek we played with the river gillie who ordered us out of the river when we disturbed the spawning of the trout. This added to the fun as we continued our daily outings, keeping a watchful eye out for our tormentor. Actually, it was the other way around as my friend and I were the tormentors, the elderly gillie desperately tried to keep the river sacrosanct for the noble art of fly fishing. With the rest of the world trying to kill each other, the priorities of the gillie and the traditional establishment he protected made for an interesting comparison in values.

This delightful interlude came to an end when I was delivered to Paddington Station in London to catch the train to the school's new home in Devon. It was like a scene from the Harry Potter books with boys rushing hither and thither, porters with baggage wagons and steam everywhere. Lots of steam. In my school uniform, my sister delivered me to the appropriate platform for the school train that would whisk us away to yet another new experience far from our families. It was all somewhat disturbing for a six-year-old to face on his own. The big London station with half of its glass roof blown away by the bombing was a scene of confusion: many of the trains leaving the station were carrying school children from London as thousands of evacuees headed for unknown destinations in remote parts of the country.

While voluntary, the government evacuation scheme was devised to take young children away from the dangers of the bombing in central London. It was a wrenching experience for both the mothers and the children. With their names written on a baggage label pinned to their coats and clutching their gas masks and a few personal belongings, boys and girls from the ages of three to fifteen were dispatched to an unfamiliar and frightening future away from all that they had known of family life. As you can imagine, there were many tears and hugs on the platforms of each of the London railway stations on the west and north sides of London as the city was emptied of its children. Thoughts of the Pied Piper of Hamlin might well have been brought to mind at the scene unfolding on those platforms.

At least my school mates and I were in the company of the teachers we had got to know already so there were fewer tears on our platform. Nonetheless, we were all headed for a place we had never seen and it was many miles from the south east of England that most of us called home. Yes, there was a lot of anxiety but also excitement as friends and classmates were reunited after our unexpected two-week vacation.

After a three-hour train ride, our teachers urged us to look out of the left hand windows of the train as we approached the end of our journey. From the bottom of the Taw Valley we were able to see our future home. Located on the top of a rise on the south side of the valley, Tawstock Court occupied an imposing position overlooking the 14th century village church of St. Peter's and the River Taw. It was a large white country house estate spread wide over the hillside. It presented an attractive and welcoming facade. Its roofline was crenelated with parapets which inspired the wide-eyed boys to exclaim "It's a castle". This was an exaggeration in fact but immediately appealed to the impressionable boys who loved to make up games involving knights, damsels in distress and dragons. It was a pleasant distraction from the constant war games we usually played. The first sight of our new home was encouraging.

Tawstock Court is a small stately home first built in 1574. It burned down in 1787 leaving only the watch tower and the entrance gateway standing. It was rebuilt and modernized between the years 1787 and 1800. It had been the ancestral home of the Bourchier Wrey family but the last baronet to live there leased it to St. Michaels in 1939. It stayed as a school until 2012 when tough economic times caused the school to close. It was then sold to a private owner who has stated that he intends it to revert to being a private residence. Maybe. I understand the new owner made his fortune developing real estate property.

Life in the new premises was part routine school studies and part pioneer work. There were no playing fields but there was a sheep pasture that had potential. Sheep graze turf very low rather like a mower so the turf was in relatively good condition for a cricket pitch. There were, however, large clumps of stinging nettles throughout the field. It was a case of all hands to the wheel as we were lined up across the field and instructed to pull out all weeds including the nettles.

The headmaster demonstrated that if you clasp a nettle plant firmly in your hand it does not sting you. With much trepidation, all hundred or so boys advanced in line abreast across the field tearing out the nettles and other weeds. To our surprise, the headmaster was right. The old English saying, "to grasp the nettle" meaning to be bold, proved to be valid advice. Those of us who were too timid to take this bold action were stung by the hairs

Tawstock Court. A private residence again today.

on the nettle. Fortunately, there were also plenty of Dock leaves growing in the field and this antidote to the stings was used liberally. You could say that this was a good introduction to an education in botany. It is true that if you are unflinching and grasp a stinging nettle firmly it does not sting you, even using bare hands. If you are reticent and your skin just brushes the hairs on its leaves, it will sting. Within a week, we had that field cleared of weeds

Next to be taken care of were all the sheep droppings. For this, we were issued rakes and shovels. Compared to the nettles, this was a stinky but easy job. The turf was lumpy and bore the hoof prints of the sheep. There was a big horse-drawn iron roller abandoned in a corner of the field. We had no horse to pull it so a dozen or so ten-year-olds got between the shafts and slowly the creaky old roller was hauled out of the weeds. Up and down the field, this human-powered farm implement started to flatten out the turf.

The Atco lawn mowers had been brought from the previous school grounds. With the very limited petrol ration the school had been allocated, the mowers set to work to tame the sheep pasture. These were not the perfect, pristine lawns that we were used to, but with repeated cuttings the rough clover and orchard grass pasture soon became tamed to more closely resemble the smooth surfaces of a cricket pitch. The final step was to mark out the twenty-two yards stretch of the actual wicket with the stumps at each end. The white chalk markings were easily applied and the circle of the boundary followed suit. The transformation from sheep pasture to cricket field was complete. Sort of.

Within three weeks of arrival at Tawstock, the first cricket match was played against the local village boys' team. The ball still took some unexpected bounces and fielders in the outfield sometimes slipped where the recently ousted sheep had left their protest mark. The score was unimportant. The cricket field was born and a feast of tea and cakes celebrated the effort of the boys who had made this possible. Yet another example of the wartime spirit of where there's a will there's a way, and to use the popular phrase we 'made do and mended'.

School classes were resumed from day one but all of us found it hard to concentrate when there was so much to be

Watch Tower at Tawstock Court in which we find our swords..

discovered in the grounds and old buildings. A friend and I went exploring one day and came across the old fortified stone watch tower. This was a relic from when the house was first built in 1564. To our surprise, the creaky old iron bound door was not locked. With our hearts in our mouths we lifted the bar blocking the entrance and crept in to the dark interior. Pigeons startled us as they took off from the dark recesses above with the loud clapping of wings. The smell of hundreds of bats and their droppings added to the gloom and antiquity of the old tower. Thoughts of vampires crossed our minds. Our inclination was to turn and run but curiosity prevailed. We stepped forward into the interior and slowly our eyes became accustomed to the dark. The shaft of light from the open doorway illuminated an empty chamber. Or was it empty? In one corner, there was a pile of discarded furniture and an old chest. Our luck held as we lifted the lid. It was not locked. Inside we found what can only be described as treasure to two small boys accustomed to playing at knights in armour.

Inside something heavy was wrapped in a cloth, probably an old curtain. We lifted the bundle out of the chest and unwrapped the folds. To our delight, we discovered a pair of matched swords. There was also an heraldic shield. It is probable that this was a pair of crossed swords and shield which at some point had been mounted on one of the walls of the house, more as decoration than weapons. No matter, to us this find was indeed treasure. In our imagination, these were the swords used by medieval knights in battle, maybe even in 1066 at the Battle of Hastings which we had just learned about in history class.

With a cry of "On Guard!", we quickly began our first sword fight. The swords were a bit rusty and the blades were probably quite blunt but there was no doubt they were dangerous weapons. They were heavy for us and we thrust and parried with a two-handed grip. It was too dark in the tower for a real sword fight so we emerged into the sunlight to continue our fight to the death.

Our shouts of joy and battle screams swiftly brought several school mates to witness this clash of knights in mortal combat.

It was only a matter of a few minutes before one of the teachers heard the commotion. It was only a few more minutes before our duel was brought to an end, the swords confiscated and the door to the stone tower was shut and bolted. Never mind, D'Artagnon and I had had our moment of glory. We had made the discovery. We had actually had a real sword fight. We were heroes in our minds' eyes and enjoyed a brief moment of admiration among our school mates. It was enough excitement to dream about for the next few weeks. Gone were the usual Germans versus the British modern war games that we usually played. We were back in medieval times when men were real men and fought the honourable way, face to face and sword to sword.

By 1941, the shortages of little things had become apparent. Packaging for the everyday products we needed disappeared. Toothpaste tubes came unboxed; soap bars no longer came wrapped. School books were handed down from one year's class to the next with the bindings constantly being re-glued. Paper envelopes were saved to be slit open and the reverse side used for writing. Toilet paper frequently ran out and torn up newspapers appeared in the lavatory cubicles replacing that unique British invention, Bronco toilet paper. Relatively useless as bum wipes, the torn-off sections of Bronco made excellent tracing paper. You could see through it and the paper was smooth enough to take a pencil outline. It was beloved by budding artists more for this purpose than for what its manufacturer had intended.

The new toys were simply not available but, fortunately, the toys produced before WWII were built to last. Miniature airplanes, war vehicles, toy soldiers and realistic models of the latest weapons were constantly being traded. Dinky Toy cars were of sound construction and, even if one wheel was missing, they still performed well and had a high trading value. There was an ideal road network along the many stone balustrades in the formal gardens at Tawstock Court. The gardens were laid out in a series of terraces each with decorative yet functional stone balustrades at a perfect three-foot height. The top consisted of a flat stone surface about a foot wide, perfect for playing with toy cars. Groups of boys laid claim to different sections of these stone roadways for the free-time pursuit of playing garages, roadway management and building bomb-proof shelters for our model cars and trucks of domestic and military vehicles.

The climate of Devon is mild and wet. These are perfect conditions for the growth of moss. We were able to peel off great lengths of this natural material from the old trees and rotting stumps in the nearby woods. With the durability of turf but with one tenth the weight, this was ideal building material for the creation of garages, warehouses and even underground bunkers for our vehicles and roadways. We went as far as to create landing strips and airplane hangars for our air force of model Spitfires, Messerschmitts and other planes of both air forces. The potential for our war games on and about those stone balustrades was endless. And so were the hours we idled away there, totally absorbed in the make-believe games at which children are so adept.

By postwar standards, we were deprived of the choice of playthings. But we were rich in all that was needed to provide the endless entertainment that creative minds and a few basic materials can provide. In some respects, we were more fortunate than many peacetime children as we had a very clear vision of the bad guys and the good guys in the games we played. We had all the cast we needed to create an endless stream of plots reflecting the real-life drama being enacted elsewhere in the world, well removed from our insulated life.

The original building at Tawstock Court had been replaced with a more up-to-date residence. The tower was still standing and also the original main gate. This was a fine stone entrance-way, complete with a portcullis gate that could be lowered up and down by a system of rope pulleys. This was, of course, locked in the open position as soon as we arrived on the scene.

We were able to use our pocket money to buy a tennis ball each for a penny or so. Most boys owned one and promptly wrote their name on the fuzzy surface. We invented all manner of games with the balls but the most popular one involved bouncing the balls off the carved surface of the entrance wall. The wall was covered with stone carvings of gargoyles, heraldic shields and decorative filigree designs carved in stone. It was a very uneven surface full of indentures. The rules of the ball game were complex and changed frequently but always required the ball to hit specific features each with different point values. Inevitably, the balls would become jammed into the various grooves of the carvings. By the end of each week the gateway would be festooned with the yellow balls. It no longer resembled the formal entrance to a stately home. You could be forgiven if you assumed a German fighter plane had strafed it with yellow bullet holes or perhaps the stonework had mysteriously developed a bad case of chicken pox.

It became a tradition that every Saturday after morning classes Sam, the school porter, would lean a ladder against the wall and pick out the tennis balls. He would throw them down to cheers from the students waiting below. There would then be a scramble to determine their various owners. No sooner had the ladder been removed than the wall would be peppered again with the tennis balls and the process would start over again. To their credit, the staff tolerated this practice and it soon became established as a St. Michaels' tradition.

The surrounding woods were a great source of entertainment. We would form small groups or gangs and build houses or forts in the undergrowth. All pupils were members of one of four school groups or houses named Druids, Elizabethans, Singhalese and a fourth one which I believe may have had the dull name of "School House". In the "wilderness", members of the group would select sites in the same neighbourhood largely for protection from marauders from other houses. Each group of friends or 'family' within each house would construct walls and entrances from the natural material available in the woods around us. Manufactured material such as wooden boards were not permitted. Each community of homes developed an interesting social system. In many ways, it was an early form of what later became known as a Hobbit village. The Laurel tree grew in the local woods. Laurel leaves are waxy and long-lasting so they became the currency of the community. Some homes would be shops and would trade in make-believe commodities. Other homes offered services of one kind or another. All of which was pure fantasy but came to be important in the wilderness games we played in that precious hour or so after school each day.

Raids on each other's communities were frequent and prisoners were taken. Each school group had its own shouted calls to warn of impending raids and to summon the 'troops'. When the bell was rung, sounding an end to this free time in the woods, the games would cease and no lingering attitudes or achievements were carried back into the school. The next day would be a fresh start. This social fantasy had interesting implications. Somewhere in the psychology of the games there were undertones of 'The Lord of the Flies', reflections of the family life we no longer had and the mentality of a people at war.

During the school terms, there were times when those students who had stayed out of trouble were given half-day holidays and were taken by train or bus to the beaches. There are some lovely seaside villages in North Devon. Our favourites were Biddeford, Croyd Bay and Clovelly. Unlike south and south-east England, there was plenty of beach access where the sands had not been mined. Invasion by German forces was deemed impractical and, therefore, unlikely along this rugged coast.

The village of Clovelly is well-known for its steep main street that leads down into the harbour. It is so steep that vehicles cannot use the road. Instead donkeys and even wooden sleds were used to haul commercial goods up and down to the shops. There was a lifeboat station at the foot of the street on the beachfront. On a visit there one summer's day, a plane was seen to crash into the sea a mile or two offshore near the Isle of Lundy. The call went out for all available folk to help launch the lifeboat. There was no shortage of volunteers among my school mates. The launching was relatively easy as the lifeboat was on a steep ramp leading down from its station just above the beach. With a rush, the large boat rolled on its wheeled carriage rapidly down the ramp into the sea creating a huge wave. With the engine already running, the craft immediately sped out to sea on its mission of rescue. Whether the pilot of the plane was English or German was of no concern, as there was a soul to be saved.

The return part of the lifeboat's journey was more difficult as it had to be hauled up the steep ramp back into its housing in readiness for the next mission. While we were kept well back from the forefront of the activity, the thirty or so of us who were there helped pull on the long ropes that hauled the lifeboat back up the ramp. We enjoyed participating in the excitement of a real rescue at sea and felt proud to have been able to help.

My time at St. Michaels was pleasant enough but, being so far away, I really missed my family. That I had been sent away at such a young age may also have been a factor. I would go home for each of the holidays and be reminded of how I missed family life. Going back to school after the holidays was always a traumatic experience. My sisters took turns in escorting me back to Paddington Station for the school train and they disliked the experience as much as I did. It was not that they were sad to see me go. Oh no. Every time I would embarrass them with the tantrums I would throw on the platform. Parents would look on in horror as I threw my cap under the train and lay kicking and screaming on the platform. However, my bad behaviour eventually had the desired effect and I was withdrawn from the school in 1942. Instead, I was enrolled in King's School in Rochester. This day school was just a fifteen-minute train ride from home.

With hindsight, I believe my education benefited from the change of school as King's was well-established, with a good academic reputation and provided more complete facilities than St. Michaels could offer. It happened to be the second oldest school in England, having been founded in the year 608 when it was established at the same time as Rochester Cathedral. My father was educated there some forty years before me. Most importantly, many of my friends from home were also pupils so I immediately felt at home. It was especially helpful that my best pal, Richard, was also attending. He was a year older than me and in a class ahead of mine. He and I were able to take the train to school together and he made my days as a new student easier for me as I got to know the ropes.

At this point I was a much happier boy.

Knees Up, Mother Brown

Knees up Mother Brown
Knees up Mother Brown
Under the table you must go
Ee-aye, Ee-aye, Ee-aye-oh
If I catch you bending
I'll saw your legs right off
Knees up, knees up
don't get the breeze up
Knees up Mother Brown

The war years spawned an unexpected benefit: the music and entertainment industry thrived. The singers, comedians and storytellers stepped into the breach caused by the stresses of wartime conditions to fill the huge demand for comfort and emotional fulfillment. There was a pattern to this artistic smorgasbord.

Jingoism and inspiring nationalism was a major theme of many of the popular songs. Wherever people were assembled, whether in the armed forces, in the air raid shelters or in the factories or meeting halls, the crowds would be inspired to sing rousing songs such as "Knees Up, Mother Brown" or, in a more nationalistic vein, "There'll Always Be an England." There was no need to orchestrate the response of a crowd as it was an automatic reaction to being together. Joining in the communal singing with a crowd of fellow citizens created a sense of security, unity and courage.

Clear and easy-to-remember lyrics were important. Repetition of both the melody and the words was helpful to people who, under other circumstances, would not be able to carry a tune and would probably be too shy to sing along. That's why such rousing, fun and simple tunes as "Knees Up Mother Brown" were so popular. This particular song dates back to at least WWI, when crowds were singing and dancing to it on Armistice Night in 1918. It is a traditional Cockney song with the words 'knees up' referring to a dance party. Although part of Cockney lore, it wasn't until 1938 when the words and music were published. It seemed very appropriate that it should become so popular again in WWII. It is also interesting to note that this tune was the inspiration for the song and dance routine named "Step in Time" in the Hollywood movie "Mary Poppins". Apparently, Walt Disney himself was seen singing and dancing to it on the set in Hollywood during the production of the film; such was its infectious power to get everyone who heard it to join in. It was the perfect antidote to all the trials and stresses of wartime Britain.

The list of all the popular songs of the war years is huge. It is likely that more tunes were written in these seven years than in any other period of an equal length. There were three main themes which seemed to run through music during that time. The first category of songs was designed to rouse patriotism, to unite the people and build confidence. "There'll Always Be an England" was the epitome of this genre.

I give you a toast Ladies and gentlemen
I give you a toast Ladies and gentlemen
May this fair land we love so well

In Dignity and freedom dwell
While worlds may change and go awry
There'll always be an England
While there's a country lane
Wherever there's a cottage small
Beside a field of grain

In a more intimate mood, many nostalgic love songs were crafted to appeal to the individual rather than to the crowd. The purpose of the lyrics was not necessarily to appeal to a sweetheart or lover but often referred to a way of life from which ordinary people had been disconnected by the war. In a trench in a foreign land or being tossed about in rough seas on the ocean; the thoughts of home, family, and an existence contrasting with the rigours of the current situation had a huge appeal to those separated from their families. Many people found themselves alone in a harsh world and were homesick for the former life they knew and loved. Songs with this theme were just as moving as those love ballads written for a sweetheart left behind. Good examples of this type of tune were "Keep the Home Fires Burning", written by Ivor Nevello in 1914 and revived again in 1940. Then there was "We'll Meet Again", made popular by Vera Lynn. Both of these tunes, among many others, exemplified the craving for a return to normalcy in a tempestuous and hostile world torn apart by war.

The third genre could be defined as cheeky and irreverent. These ditties made the most of the British sense of humour and indirectly poured scorn on the phlegmatic German character. Belittling the enemy in this way had the effect of building up one's own confidence. Humour becomes an important ingredient in lyrics designed with this end in mind. The queen of this type of song was Gracie Fields with her engaging Yorkshire accent and her sense of the ridiculous. Some examples of such comic songs were "Walter, Walter Lead Me to the Altar" and "The Biggest Aspidistra in the World". On a more nostalgic note, her song "Wish Me Luck as You Wave Me Goodbye" was a direct reference to the anxieties of the troops.

A couple of male entertainers of the time were George Formby and Arthur Askey. Neither of them could be described as heartthrob celebrities. They both portrayed little guys from next door. They were of the people. It was their cheeky humour that endeared them to their audiences. Arthur Askey's rendition of "Hang Out the Washing on the Siegfried Line" 'cocked a snoot' at the Germans. George Formby's "When I'm Cleaning Windows" combined humour with the nearest thing to a sexy theme that the morals of the time would allow. Happy and cheerful were the two ingredients in the recipe for their success.

The songs of the day were not confined to British singers. Even before the war, the American entertainers had a following within the British audiences. With the arrival of American troops in 1943 and the advent of A.F.N., the American Forces Network, the more upbeat offerings of the Hollywood entertainers were quick to catch on. The Andrews Sisters were perhaps the best known of the US songsters. With catchy tunes like "Boogie Woogie Bugle Boy" and "Don't Sit Under the Apple Tree", their music lit up most of the 'dance hops' held regularly to entertain the troops.

Other American entertainers were Jo Stafford singing "You Belong to Me", Doris Day with "Sentimental Journey", and Louis Armstrong playing "I Wonder". This was a time of many artists touring to entertain the troops. Notable among them were Bing Crosby, Bob Hope, Spike Jones, Phil Silvers and many others too numerous to mention. American songs seemed to be very directly crafted to get to the point in the typical American way--titles such as "Kiss the Boys Goodbye" and "Praise the Lord and Pass the Ammunition" need little explanation.

It was the era of the Big Band: Tommy Dorsey, Benny Goodman, Duke Ellington and others. Perhaps the best known of these was Glenn Miller and his orchestra. Miller was commissioned to form the US Army Air Force Band in 1942. His band quickly became popular with the Allied Forces and the British public. Pieces such as "In the Mood" and "Chattanooga Choo Choo" quickly became big hits. The Glenn Miller Orchestra with its military connections made many broadcasts from right behind the front lines of the fighting forces.

This risky exposure eventually led to the tragic loss of Glenn Miller in December 1944. Officially, Glenn Miller was listed as 'missing in action' and presumed dead. The story of his loss remains a mystery.

On December 15th, 1944 Glenn Miller set out in a single engine Norseman plane of the US Army Air Force from Bedford in England headed to Paris for a performance in the liberated city. His plane was reported missing and presumed crashed somewhere over the English Channel. No remains of the plane or its passengers were ever found. In attempting to solve the mystery three possible scenarios have been presented.

The first possibility is that his plane was hit by one or more unexploded bombs dropped by a formation of 138 Lancaster bombers of the R.A.F. returning from an aborted sortie due to bad weather over Germany. Official reports confirm that as many as 100,000 incendiary bombs had been dropped in a designated safe area in the North Sea. It was the practice of such bombers to jettison their payload safely at sea because the planes were unable to land with the bombs still on board. A navigator on one of the planes reported that he had seen a small plane spiralling down into the sea.

The second theory is based on a report by an anti-aircraft gunner stationed in Folkestone. He believed that his battery shot down the plane. Thus, Glenn Miller was the victim of 'friendly fire', a tragedy which was not uncommon.

The third possibility was suggested by a German journalist after the war that Glenn Miller actually made it safely to Paris. The journalist based his conclusions on confidential American reports that he obtained in Washington through the Freedom of Information Act. His research went on to suggest that Glenn Miller died of a heart attack during a relationship with a Parisian prostitute. He further claims that the US Army covered up the incident in order to protect the reputation of the bandleader.

None of these three postulations can be proven. It seems unlikely that the small plane would have flown over the North Sea as the direct route from Bedford to Paris would not normally have taken him that far east. A direct flight to Paris would likely have taken his plane over or near Folkestone but the gunner's report was not specific enough to be convincing. The third option of the heart attack in Paris was possible but the journalist may have been looking for a good story for his paper and based his conclusions on rumour only.

Whatever the truth, it seems that Glenn Miller was a victim of friendly fire of one sort or another.

Entertainment, of course, was not limited to music and song. The broadcasts on the radio also encompassed comedy and play acting or storytelling. Perhaps the most popular radio show of all was *It's That Man Again* or I.T.M.A., featuring Tommy Handley, Jack Train, Hattie Jacques and other actors with scripts written by Ted Kavanagh. That *'Man'* referred to Hitler. The humorous scripts were often written just before the show was to go on air and included up-to-the-minute skits on the day's news. Every Friday night large audiences huddled around the radio for their weekly fix of the inanities of I.T.M.A. The programme relied heavily on catchphrases that the audience could predict hearing every time one of the characters was introduced into a sketch. With no particular plot, the principle characters included Mona Lot, the laundry lady (it's being so cheerful as keeps me going), Mrs. Mopp (Can I do you now, Sir') and Colonel Chinstrap the drunken retired Indian Army officer (Don't mind if I do). Other catchphrases included 'I go, I come back' (Ali Oop), 'This is Funt speaking', the German spy, and the acronym *TTFN* (Ta Ta For Now), which quickly became a figure of speech used by the public in everyday language.

Variety shows have always been popular with British audiences and were a feature of much of the broadcast entertainment. *In Town Tonight* was always amusing and introduced celebrities in interviews and clips from their shows. Henry Hall's one hour variety programme was a feature on a weekly basis. *London After Dark* was a similar show in the later years in which the glamour of the stage and film personalities brightened the lives of ordinary folk.

Other programmes which became popular were *Dick Barton, Special Agent*, who solved all manner of crimes in quick-fire order and *Into Battle*, a five-minute re-enactment of a battleground scenario. With a very different tone, the daily *Children's Hour* at 5 pm. was one programme I was allowed to listen to before doing school homework and other chores. Quiz shows were always popular with *Twenty Questions* standing out in my memory. On the news front, Richard Dimbleby was the best-known reporter, frequently broadcasting from just behind the front lines in battle. And, of course, the daily newscasts at 9 pm. drew huge audiences. The news presenters' measured tones added gravity, reassurance and the perception of truth to the material they had to impart regardless of the dramatic information of the day or the government spin that just might be included.

WWII was the first war in which there was one medium that could reach virtually all of the public almost instantly. Despite all its faults, perceived or real, the British Broadcasting Corporation played a major part in the war effort of the nation.

Bomb Proof!

The bombing raids were hazardous enough for people but they were even more of a danger to animals, both wild and domestic. At least the people knew what was going on and could take appropriate shelter. The animals had to take their chances in the open air or under whatever natural protection they could find. Domestic pets were usually cared for, and taken into shelter by their owners, but the farm animals and the true wildlife were on their own. I do not recall many instances in which our farm animals were injured but there were some cases. One incident does stand out as it was close to home and recalled humorously.

My father liked to ride a horse and spent many happy hours riding with the local pack of hounds before war was declared. With the outbreak of war, most fox hunting ceased and many good horses were turned out to pasture for the duration of the hostilities. In the First World War, most horses were requisitioned and went to France to serve with the troops. Very few returned alive. In WWII, the army did not need horses for war duty other than for a few specialized uses. This was fortunate for my father's favourite hunter. He was a tall 17 hand chestnut gelding, who carried my father well across country. His name was Sandboy. He was destined for a life of idleness while we got on with fighting the enemy.

I remember when Sandboy was pastured out in the field we called 'the meadow'. He enjoyed his full-time freedom and grew comfortably plump in the meantime. He was considered 'bomb proof', as the saying goes in the horse world. He was a safe ride because he did not react to unexpected and startling incidences while being ridden. Now he had to prove this in reality since our home was on the flight path of the German bombers on their way to London. With that innate ability that all animals have, he soon adjusted to the bangs and flashes of the nightly air raids as the bombers passed overhead. There was a chance that he could be injured by exploding bombs but the real risk was the amount of shrapnel falling out of the sky from the anti-aircraft guns stationed in the vicinity.

It is true that we had a stable for him, which would have given him protection but we didn't have the time to devote to a horse that was not being ridden. So Sandboy spent the days and nights idling in his pasture in all but the worst weather. This suited him fine as all horses prefer the freedom and access to unlimited grazing of a field, compared to the confinement of a stable. Nor was he alone. My sister Helen's mare, Cider, enjoyed the same freedom so he did not lack companionship.

One morning we went to check how the horses were after a particularly noisy night only to find a long slashing wound diagonally across the knee of Sandboy's hind leg. A jagged piece of an exploded shell had caught him in its descent to earth.

Fortunately, no bones were broken but it was a proud wound and the flesh opened up around the bone. It had happened sometime during the night and it was important to get it attended to before infection set in. We managed to get him to hobble back to his stable and cleaned the wound as best as we could but it needed stitching up. This posed a problem in the wartime conditions of 1942; the local veterinarian had been called up for duties elsewhere. What to do?

In the village, we still had a local doctor. Our Dr. Hasler was getting on in years but still was a dab hand at delivering babies. In fact, he successfully home-delivered all six of my siblings and me. Each time another baby was due, the drawing room in the house was converted into a dedicated birthing room. This made life easier for all the family as it was a convenient room on the ground floor and close to kitchen and bathroom facilities. A week after each birth, the furniture would be moved around again and in the evenings the family would assemble there to hear the latest war news on the radio, to enjoy games of bridge and all the other family activities.

Dr. Hasler was quite capable of handling life's routine health requirements and ordinary misfortunes. He was there for first aid but the more serious injuries resulting from enemy action were whisked off by ambulance to the local hospital. We called to see if he could help with our war victim. Fortunately, he was in his surgery. He arrived as quickly as he could, carrying the iconic doctor's gladstone bag and puffing a little due to his advancing years.

He quickly determined the situation. We had to sedate the horse in order to stitch up the jagged wound. Sedating a 17 hand, 1200 lbs. horse was somewhat off the dosage charts for a doctor accustomed to sedating 180 lbs. humans. So, he just kept injecting the appropriate drugs and finally the big fellow slumped down on a thick bed of straw on the floor of his stable. Quickly, the stitches were sewn and the bleeding stopped.

"Well," said the good doctor, "that's a start but we need to immobilize the leg otherwise he will pop out the stitches. We will have to use a splint and put the leg in a plaster cast."

This had to be done before the anaesthetic wore off and another needle was given just to be on the safe side. A quick dash across the village green and the doctor returned with all the Plaster of Paris he could find in his surgery. Half an hour later, having used two broken broom handles as splints, the three of us covered in white plaster, put a blanket over Sandboy's head and sat on its edges to keep him down in case he came to before the plaster dried.

Eventually, Sandboy emerged from his sleep and struggled to his feet, causing just minor cracks in his plaster. A quick repair job to the plaster and he stood there wondering what this weight was doing on his hind leg. Of course, it was too much to expect the horse to accept this huge white growth and within a day or two he managed to kick off most of the cast. However, enough of the stitches held and the wound began to heal leaving behind a large scar.

My brother Robert (left) on Tommy, aged 30,
and my father (right) atop Sandboy.

Our good doctor returned to stitching up smaller patients, dispensing aspirin, and delivering babies. Sandboy was soon able to return to his life of leisure in his favourite meadow.

By the time the war ended three years later, Sandboy had survived two falling bombs that left large craters in his ten-acre pasture and an unexploded anti-aircraft shell, which had to be dug up and detonated by the bomb disposal squad. In 1944, toward the end of the war, he survived near misses by the V1 flying bombs which regularly flew overhead, sometimes crashing and exploding just a mile or two away.

Even more startling was a rogue anti-aircraft barrage balloon that lost its hydrogen and descended like a limp elephant into his paddock. As it came down, the anchor cable, which came down with it, snaked across his paddock and crossed some high voltage electric power cables. This sent sparks flying in every direction before blowing the electric power in the village. Throughout it all Sandboy and Cider, his companion horse, maintained their composure and survived without another scratch.

By 1945 you could say that Sandboy was definitely a bomb proof horse!

Eventually the war was over but Sandboy's hunting days with it. He was able to be ridden despite a rather stiff leg. My father rode him around the farm on Sundays inspecting and checking the crops and animals. This became a family tradition. I, too, can remember some gentle rides on him in the countryside as a 12-year-old boy. As you might expect, he was a very safe ride as nothing would startle him. This was just as well because it was a long way down for a 12-year-old if a mishap should occur. Yes, he was a gentle soul and indeed a bomb-proof horse, handling with equanimity whatever the war or traffic could throw at him.

Best Pals

It seemed as though I was constantly on the move between schools and school locations. Being away at boarding school in term time and then back home again for the short holidays meant that I was always coming or going. It was the same for many people in wartime. The life that people led was always on the move between the tumultuous years from 1939 to 1945.

Whereas the trauma of war encouraged the formation of friendships, it is probably true to say that these relationships were easily made but short-lived and light in nature rather than long-lasting and deep. It was not until I started at Kings School in Rochester that I had the chance to form a deeper and permanent bond with one or more other boys. Richard and I hit it off well from the moment we both attended the same day school.

Richard lived down the hill, a quarter of a mile away from our house. We lived at the top of Hook Green, the second of the two village greens in the village. Richard's home was at the bottom of the green, on the way to the railway station. Usually, I would meet up with him as the two of us ran to catch the 8:15 morning train to school. Richard was a year older than me and was in a form ahead of me at school. His prior knowledge of the school was a great help to me in settling into the new routine.

Richard's father was in banking but right from an early age Richard knew that he wanted to be a farmer. My father recognized and encouraged him in his ambitions. We were good pals but that one year advantage meant that if the opportunity arose to work on some farm project he took it, and I would find myself without my regular chum. From this early start, Richard developed into one of Britain's most knowledgeable and experienced farmers. Some years later, he was awarded the Nuffield Scholarship and spent six months in New Zealand studying agricultural methods there. Other trips included traveling through Canada and the U.S. on similar missions. Richard learned his craft through practical experience and self-study rather than through any formal college training. In his early twenties, he bought a small farm in Surrey and progressively enlarged his farming enterprise as opportunities arose in other parts of England. He served on several agricultural boards and as an advisor to agricultural groups. He and his wife Margaret eventually retired to a lovely country property near Hereford.

But all of that came later. When Richard was not answering the call of the farm, he and I basically just hung out together. We would spend our days climbing trees to add to our collections of birds' eggs. When the Land Army girls were working on the farm, we would spy on them and bug them every way we could imagine. This marked our first stirrings of interest in girls even though these ladies were old enough to be our mothers. Living on a farm, there was no mystery about the reproductive habits of the animals but when it came to girls we were as naive as any boys of that age and era. Such was our curiosity that we invited a neighbour's daughter, Jane, to come bird nesting with us. With many salacious giggles, we put the ladder we were using up against a tall tree where there was a woodpecker's nest in a hole in the trunk. Yes, we wanted to add woodpecker eggs to our collections but there was more to it than that. We invited Jane to climb up the ladder while we held it steady for her. The real purpose, of course, was to look up her skirt.

I suspect Jane was in on the game herself. She was an Admiral's daughter living next to Richard's house. I can only wonder if she is still around today and remembers this harmless but significant incident.

Our interest and explorations into the subject of girls continued more in the abstract than in any physical form. We continued with our more innocent play such as swinging on a rope in the barn and letting go at just the right moment to land in a large pile of straw. We spent many hours in that stack of straw where we kept a secret nest hidden from view. When anyone entered the barn, we kept totally silent for fear of having our den discovered. I realize now that my older brothers and sisters knew what we were up to as they had probably acted in the same way a few years earlier.

In our secret hideaway, we kept a store of our favourite items. We had a stash of comic books. *Beano and Boys Own* were our favourites. There was an active trade in the village and at school in swapping comics that we had already read for ones we had not seen. Most were pre-war editions and as time progressed the copies became more and more tattered. Nonetheless they remained precious trading items of differing values depending on the name of the comic. Copies of *Beano* were the most in demand and, therefore, of high trading value.

Not all our printed matter was quite so innocent. In quiet tones with other boys of our age, we learned about some of the sexier books that could be found usually hidden under beds or under the socks in a drawer. Three titles circulating at that time that I can remember were *No Orchids for Miss Blandish*, *Forever Amber*, and *Lady Chatterley's Lover*. By later standards, these were very mild books and despite our attempts to gather essential details from them, they left us with many unanswered anatomical blanks. One or two typed sheets did make the rounds which were a little more specific but we still longed to learn about the real thing. We did obtain a copy of a magazine for naturists but unflattering photos of unclothed regular people did nothing for us. We approached one or two girls about our age to give us a showing but we had no success on this score.

Finally, we had to admit defeat in our search for knowledge and had to be satisfied with playing 'Doctor'. Since this was wartime, most of our Doctor experiences involved pretending to remove a bullet from each other. This little scenario was because we heard that the first bomb that fell in the village injured a woman and rumour had it that a piece of the bomb injured her in the behind. To us small boys, this was titillating. The fact that it was her bum was more important than the fact that she was injured. Such are the minds of boys at that age and from what I can gather playing Doctor is a rite of passage encountered by most of our kind at a certain age.

It seems that all boys are fascinated with weapons. Perhaps the most intriguing of these is the bow and arrow. Guns and swords are OK but there is more romance to the bow and arrow. We read in the history books that the best bows were made of yew wood and the wood of choice for arrows was holly. These are both relatively rare trees in southern England and even if you do find a yew tree it is difficult to cut the required shape for a bow. Holly trees are more numerous but they rarely produce branches that are straight enough for arrows. Nonetheless, we sought high and low for the right materials. We also needed feathers for the flights on the arrows. This was not a problem as there were chicken feathers aplenty.

We tried splitting flint stones to create sharp arrowheads. We learned the technique for doing this but were not very successful. In truth, we found it easier to go into the ploughed fields looking for real arrowheads left by our forebears, the Anglo Saxons. The soil in Kent is a mixture of chalk and flint and, even though the pointed flints we gathered were probably not the real thing, many of the shards from the flint stones were sharp and shaped reasonably well for an arrowhead. We tried splitting the heads of the arrows and binding the small flint pieces into place with fine twine and glue. Our creations looked lethal enough but rarely survived more than one shot before splitting apart. The strings for the bows were no problem. Being on a farm, there was plenty of binder twine string discarded after the straw sheaves had been cut.

Eventually, we had our bows and arrows assembled and off we two Robin Hoods strode boldly, looking for Nazis or wild game to shoot. Our first experimental shots proved to be painful. We had forgotten that the archers of olden times wore a leather forearm protector called a 'brassard' or 'bracer' to avoid the burn of the bowstring scraping the skin of the forearm. No problem: once experienced, we learned to wear long-sleeved garments or, better still, wear a gauntlet glove that protected you above the wrist. Our accuracy with the bows was poor at best. The curves in the arrows didn't help and even the slow-moving chickens we practiced on were not in any real danger.

We set up targets of painted circles on bits of old cardboard. Occasionally, with a bit of luck, we would score a hit but only at close range.

Soon the appeal of playing Robin Hood wore off and we resorted to firing our arrows, now with the flint heads missing, over the high garden wall into the neighbour's property where he had some old greenhouses. When our small supply of arrows had run out, we switched to throwing stones over the wall. We were firing blind as the garden wall was about eight feet high but we knew we had a hit when we heard the sound of breaking glass. At this point we would take off at full speed with the roar of an angry voice behind us. Since we were out of sight the owner did not know where the missiles had come from although I am sure he had a pretty good idea. Horrible miscreants that we were, our vandalism had little effect in the end as falling shrapnel and the blast from some nearby bombs eventually destroyed most of the panes of glass.

In the same category of weaponry, home-made catapults were all the rage at the time. We would cut a forked stick from the woods, scrounge an old inner tube from a car tire, and cut the rubber into strips a half inch wide. After we had lashed each end of the rubber lengths to the top of the 'Y' part of the catapult stick and threaded a piece of leather onto the centre of the rubber bands, we had ourselves the lethal weapon all boys of that age desired. All we needed after that was a collection of round pebbles in our pant pockets for ammunition and we were an armed force to be reckoned with.

There were always swarms of sparrows around the farmyard feeding on chicken feed or spilled grain. My father paid us a penny for each sparrow we killed. In the early days, we would lie in wait in the straw to take pot shots with our catapults at the flocks of sparrows. Occasionally, we were successful more by luck than skill but we had the satisfaction of adding to our pocket money.

I would like to think that our targets were limited to the sparrows but there were occasions when we engaged in warfare of a more serious kind. In the village, there were two or three informal gangs of boys. Each gang had its own territory and occasional clashes took place when territorial boundaries were overstepped. Catapults were the choice of weapons in such events but usually there was more bluster and bombast than actual combat.

There was one occasion though when matters went too far and parental justice was called in. Richard and I were playing at building forts in the newly cut hay on the village green when we got into a shouting match with what we called local yokels. This was a small group from another gang who were out looking for trouble on their bikes. Richard was piling up yet another armful of hay to heighten the fort wall when he doubled over and let out a loud shriek. I went over to check what was wrong when we noticed that his knee was bleeding. Imbedded in the flesh was the tip of a lead pellet from an air gun. I recognized it immediately as we had the same gun at home for shooting sparrows. The air gun is not a lethal weapon and the wound was relatively minor but made his knee sore. Meanwhile, the other gang members wasted no time in disappearing on their bikes.

This incident had escalated matters beyond any acceptable level. Parents got involved and called in the local bobby. I think the culprits were admonished and we all had a 'good talking to' about getting along together. The incident passed with little more being said or done. We were all urged to fight the Germans and not each other.

We considered our nest in the pile of straw in the barn to be ours and ours alone. There was one occasion when our privacy was violated by a chicken, which had fancied our location and had laid an egg alongside our treasured comics and catapults. This was not as unusual as you might expect because all our residents of the henhouse were allowed free range throughout the farmyard. Still, the chicken had violated our secluded den.

Eventually, we grew older and wiser and more conventional. Richard began to spend more time gaining experience on the farm and we spent less time together. We remained good friends but we were on different paths. He finished his school years at Kings School and I was headed back to boarding school. Again, I was following in the footsteps of my older brothers and was signed up for Malvern College, first at Harrow-On-The-Hill and then back to Malvern itself in Worcestershire. Now that I was older, and the war had come to an end, I was happy enough to go back to boarding school. I am not sure that my education benefited from going to Malvern College. Kings School was a fully functioning school throughout the war. Many of the better and younger teachers were away on active service but this was true of all schools during this time. At the war's end, good teachers came back to their chosen vocation at Kings. Going to Malvern, I entered a school that had to build itself back up after being expropriated and broken apart for the sake of the war effort, and I believe the quality of the education it offered suffered. I might have benefited more from staying on at Kings where there was less upheaval to the school system.

As a sequel to our friendship in our early days, Richard and I stayed in touch when we were both married. When my wife and I eventually left to live in Canada, he and I lost touch for many years however, in our retirement we established contact again and rekindled our friendship even though we were living in different countries. Old friends are good friends.

How We Had Fun

Young people will have fun wherever they can find it. As a group, they are more flexible than their elders and can adapt more readily. With the changed social circumstances of wartime, it was inevitable that the youth of the nation would adapt better to the shortages and travel restrictions. The emphasis for adults was to devote most of their energy to the war effort. Young people were, in one sense, set free to devise their own forms of amusement from the facilities that were still available. They were not required to contribute directly to the war effort so they tended to use their free time to develop their own entertainment. In doing so, they created new pastimes and relied more than ever on each other for fun things to do. Here are a few of the activities that kept us entertained.

The Game of "Conkers"

The first requirement was that a Horse Chestnut tree be growing in the neighbourhood. This was not a problem in most areas of England where this tree is common. Horse Chestnuts produce their glorious blooms in May and their shiny hard "conker" seeds in September.

For centuries, the autumn colours have heralded the new season for this ancient game. Any child could participate because all you needed was a piece of string about two feet long with a double knot at one end. A ripe, hard, shiny bright chestnut seed was then selected from the many on the ground beneath the trees or by knocking the ripe fruit out of the branches with a well-thrown stick. There was something sensuous about handling these shiny smooth fruits that glistened with that lovely rich chestnut tone.

Timing was important in seeking to obtain perfect conkers. Until the seeds are ripe they are encased in a prickly seed case that

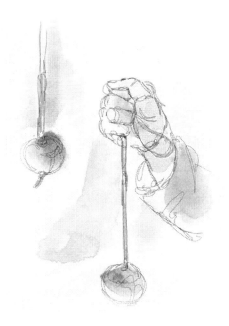

is hard to open. Inside, the fruit is still white in colour. When the seed is mature, the colour changes to a rich brown and the seed case opens up to eject the goal sought by players of this ancient game.

With the perfect conker selected, a hole was then pierced through the seed with a meat skewer or drill and the string was threaded through with the knot at the end, stopping the conker as it slid to the bottom of the string.

The object of the game was to break your opponent's conker by hitting it with yours. Each player took turns to strike at the other's conker while its owner was required to hold it still, and suspended on its string. Eventually, one of the two contesting conkers was split and knocked off its string. The intact victorious conker earned the title of being a "One-er" with the first win and then went on to become a "Two-er" with the next win and so on. It was unlikely that any conkers would get past being a "Five-er" as its owner would probably have retired it with honour by this battle-weary stage.

There was much skill involved both in terms of the selection of the right conker and in mastering the technique of the sharp, snappy hit which delivered the knock-out blow. Serious players would try gently baking their conkers in the oven to harden them but, if not done right, they became too brittle and broke apart on the first blow. Some contestants preferred their conkers to be fresh and just off the tree as these seeds were more supple and could resist hard knocks. Others chose naturally dried conkers as they were harder and shattered the opponent's offering. There was no magic formula and I suspect the key to success was more in the technique of the hit than in the condition of the conker.

The term "Conker" must have come from the dangers of a poorly swung weapon which would often miss the opponent's target and arc on its string to 'conk' the striker on the head or hand. Sore knuckles were just a hazard that keen players endured for the sake of the sport they loved to play.

Whereas the proper conker matches were genuine competitions with rules which had to be obeyed, there also existed the more violent and hurtful encounters in which conkers, picked off the ground in abundance, were used as ammunition in free-wheeling fights between gangs of youths. The damage inflicted with a well-thrown conker could smart but at least they were preferable as missiles to the other easily available weapon, a stone. There were no rules for such encounters and many were the purple bruises amongst gatherings of boys in conker season.

Kick-The-Can or "Tinny"

To play a really good game of "Kick-The-Can", you needed several players, lots of space, good hiding places and an old tin can. It was best if the playing field consisted of a garden that completely surrounded the house. This provided access to the home base for the can from more than one direction.

One person was selected to be the guardian of the tin can. Upon finding a player in hiding, the guard had to rush back to place one foot on the can, name the player in a loud voice and say "1...2...3". This made the captured player a prisoner. The objective was for the other players to release any prisoners by racing the guard back to the can, kicking it as far as possible and thus releasing all prisoners. The guardian of the tin then had to retrieve the can, place it back in position, and start trying to catch the other players all over again.

It was not often that all seven siblings in our family were together at the same time but, when you take into account that each of us had our own group of friends of approximately the same age as ourselves; it was not difficult to gather together six or eight players of assorted ages to play this age-old game.

Just about any tea-time in reasonable weather found a group of us assembled on the garden lawn fighting over who was going to be the guardian of the tin can. This was a tough position to play as there were usually enough players to keep you constantly running back to place your foot on the can and to shout out the name of the victim you had spotted. You had only to turn your back for a moment and yet another player would dart out and kick the can, shouting "Tinny", so that all the captured players could run off and hide again. We usually had to set a time limit on how long you were expected to be "It". An overly long time for some of the less adept players guarding the tin often led to frustration and tears for the younger players whose turn it was to become "It".

The Daily Egg Hunt

Whereas Kick-The-Can was played on a frequent, but irregular basis, the chore of collecting the harvest of chicken eggs on the farm was a daily event. Not only was the taste of true free-range eggs far superior to the bought kind but hunting for the hen's nests and collecting the eggs was great fun. It was really a game of hide and seek between humans and chickens.

The chickens would usually do their egg laying in the morning, so we would grab a basket and head out around the farm buildings in the afternoon. If there were any visitors around, they loved to join in on this daily event, especially visitors from the cities. We would have to look everywhere: in the hedgerows, in the straw mounds in the barn, under the horses' mangers, and even in the seats of the open top car which was laid up on blocks for the duration of the war in the big old Elizabethan barn. The smarter hens even knew enough to build their nests in a grove of stinging nettles. They did not appear to get stung but our bare legs and arms were very vulnerable when reaching in to take the eggs.

If we found a chicken still on its nest after 3 pm., it was a sure sign that she had laid a full clutch of about a dozen eggs and was sitting on them as a "broody" hen with a view to producing a family. At this stage, the eggs would be no good for eating, so we would leave her on her eggs and she would emerge after the incubation period of 21 days with a dozen little yellow balls of fluff following behind.

When a hen had laid her morning egg, she would emerge into the open and set up a loud cackling as if to say "I've done my duty, now let me get to eat". If we were around when this happened, we would make a mental note of where she had come from and check that place for eggs later in the afternoon. When a mother hen emerged with her chicks, the tone of her clucking would be very different as she constantly gave instructions 'sotto voce' to her offspring to stay in line or come and check out a good source of insects or other tasty morsels. The problem then was to try and corral the hen and family into one of the portable small hen houses in order to protect the family from the inevitable foxes, stoats, and even rats, which would range about during the night looking for an easy meal.

My mother was in charge of the poultry and I don't think she ever had to plan to breed more chickens as it all happened so naturally. The hens had a nice long life but the lives of the young cockerels were much shorter. After about three months of free ranging, the male birds would be confined to the bachelor quarters consisting of a fenced-in area. There they were fed double rations to fatten them up. As needed, one or two of them would be selected for a water-only diet for the last 24 hours of their lives. In one swift motion, their necks would be rung and they appeared on the dinner table with a few tantalizing strips of bacon sizzling over their breasts. Oh, let's not forget the white sauce made with bread crumbs simmered in milk and a whole onion with a clove stuck in it. Now that's what real roast chicken tastes like.

Cigarette Cards

In every boy's pocket, whether city or country-born, there would be one or more cigarette cards. Perhaps half a dozen all of the same series of famous cricketers held together with an elastic band or a selection of film stars or football players. A few more would be of aircraft illustrations, both friend and foe. These are a boy's trading cards, always close at hand in case someone wanted one of these in exchange for one of the cricketers or other sets he was seeking to augment his collection.

Cigarette cards were included in cigarette packages to promote sales. They were first introduced in the 19th century and continued to be very popular right up to the early days of the war when the paper they were printed on was required for the war effort. That was no discouragement to the boys collecting the cards: it added to the rarity and, therefore, the trading value of the cards from the pre-war days.

Not all the cards ended up displayed in carefully mounted collections. They had another use that made them desirable. Every boy worth his salt had a beat-up bicycle or even a hand-me-down tricycle. In the boys' games, these vehicles played the part of a tank, a jeep, an armoured personnel carrier or some other vehicle of war. The sounds these make-believe war machines made were imitated by the boys' voices but there was nothing quite like the real sound of a roaring engine as it went into battle. A good way to simulate this was by attaching a card to the frame of the bike so that the spokes of the bike wheel clipped it as the wheel turned. The constant sound of the clicking of the card was an acceptable imitation of an engine. Of course, it was tough on the card as it slowly disintegrated under the constant ripping of the spokes but it masterfully fired the imagination of a small boy.

Cigarette cards and regular playing cards also were used in a game that could be set up wherever two small boys found themselves with a few minutes of time to fill. It consisted of flipping cards against a wall. Rules varied but the general principle was to toss the cards against a wall to see if your card could capture your opponent's by landing on top of it. A simple game easily started and easily packed up when the school bell sounded.

Saucy Postcards

Among the older boys, the collecting of saucy seaside postcards was quite the rage. These were the postcards you purchased on a visit to a seaside resort and mailed home to your friends with the time-honoured saying "Wish you were here". The real appeal of the cards was the colourful cartoon illustration on the back showing some form of funny and probably sexy situation with a comment whose meaning could be taken in two different ways: innocent or saucy. Strictly nudge nudge (wink wink) stuff but risqué enough to excite adolescent boys. The printing of these cards was interrupted during the war but the older ones were still in circulation and were traded by the older boys and kept out of the sight of parents.

Lawn Cricket

The flowers in the garden at the farmhouse had a short life. With four boys in the family, there was the constant sound of leather on willow as lawn cricket often was played when two or more of us were home. The girls also joined in and my sister Mary even played on an English cricket team that toured Holland before the war.

Three stumps at the batsman's end and one stump at the bowler's end were always in position. A good drive on the off side often beheaded the tulips in spring. A boundary hit on the leg side inevitably caused a time-out as we searched for the ball in the raspberry patch in the kitchen garden. In raspberry-picking season, this often ended the cricket game as sweet-toothed appetites caused "stumps to be drawn".

These early practices paid off as my brother John played for Norfolk in the Minor Counties league after the war. I was never sure how he qualified to play for a county in which he did not reside. The fact that he scored a century in 55 minutes for Norfolk on one occasion probably earned him honourary residency status. I, too, had some success in playing for my school cricket team but this was pale in comparison to brother John's skill with bat and ball.

Marbles

Marbles is a game with distant origins. There is evidence of one form or another of this ancient game being played by the Romans and even earlier civilizations. The first marbles were made of baked clay. Today's lovely glass marbles date back to more recent times at the turn of the 19th century.

The clink of marbles bumping together in the pockets of short pants worn by school boys was heard frequently. Any location with a flat surface sufficed for an instant game between classes or during other idle moments. The rules of the game were varied but the intention was always to capture your opponent's marble by "firing" your marble with a flick of the thumb to hit your adversary's marble and to add it to your collection.

Knucklebones

This was another ancient game. Reference is made by Sophocles to the playing of the game by Greek soldiers during the Trojan War. Originally, the playing pieces were the dried-out bones of the knuckle joint from a sheep. By WWII, the pieces were made of light metal or some form of plastic. They replicated the uneven shape of the sheep bones.

I delighted in producing my set of pieces consisting of the original version. It was not difficult to find the bleached bones from a dead sheep that had been buried years ago on the farm and later dug up by foxes. On producing the bones from my pocket, I enjoyed the reactionary "Ugh!" which often followed. I felt it gave me a psychological advantage.

There were five bones in a set. The object of the game was to toss first one bone into the air, pick up a second bone while it is in the air and catch the original bone on the back of the hand. This was followed in sequence with the tossing of two bones, then three bones up to the ultimate five bones without dropping them. To end up with all five bones on the back of your hand was not easily achieved.

Group Games

One of the games we played at school was British Bulldog. This was a very simple but sometimes rough game in which one fellow was appointed "It". The rest of the players lined across one end of the designated playing area and tried to reach the other end without being grabbed by the "bulldog". If successful, the bulldog had to hold onto the victim long enough to say, "British Bulldog 123". At that point, the victim switched to becoming one of the bulldogs. This continued until the last free player was caught as he tried to make the run from one end of the area to the other.

Since this was often played in the school yard, sometimes there were cases of scraped knees, blooded noses, and even fights and tears. It was somewhat reminiscent of those movies we saw of wildebeest trying to cross the Zambezi River through crocodile-infested water. I suppose it helped to make men of boys but I doubt that school principals would allow it to be played today.

Of a somewhat more civilized nature was the game of "Capture the Flag". This was usually a school-sponsored event and was thus more controlled. In the battle between the two sides, participants were considered prisoners if an opponent managed to break a length of wool thread that was tied around a player's upper arm. This was a relatively non-violent method of capture. The winning team was the group that managed to capture the opposing team's flag without being caught.

Party Games

Wartime conditions did not inhibit the mood for parties. If anything, the external threats encouraged young people to get together more often to make their own fun at home. My friend Richard's grandfather had a fabulous party room above the garage at his house known as Maycroft. Birthdays, end of school terms or the regular public holidays were all we needed as an excuse to gather there with our friends. Our parties were innocent enough with food and games the order of the day.

"Postman's Knock" was a titillating game that always raised a little apprehension. Boys and girls would sit in a circle on the floor and the game started with "spin the bottle". An empty bottle in the middle of the circle was spun around on its side. When it stopped spinning, the boy or girl it pointed at was required to leave the room and become the Postman. The bottle was spun again and the next person of the opposite sex it pointed at was selected to be the recipient of a letter. The person waiting outside the room would then knock on the door and the youngster of the opposite sex the bottle had selected was required to go out and receive the letter. This really meant the victim was to be kissed by the boy or girl who had first been selected. This was accompanied by much catcalling from the others inside the party room. You can imagine the terror in the mind of a ten-year-old boy having to kiss a girl, not of his choosing, unseen yes, but still very much in the presence of his friends.

A little less intimidating was the game of "Pass the Orange" (or perhaps an apple as oranges were not often available). Two lines of young people were formed in a boy/girl sequence. The orange was placed under the chin of the first in line and had to be passed on down the line without it being dropped. The first team to get the orange to the end of the line was the winner but really the objective was to enjoy the contortions and the intimacy of the participants as the orange passed down the line under people's chins. As often as not, the orange would begin to slip down from under the chin and would have to be pursued downwards by the partner with only his or her neck and chin being allowed as the transfer device. Again, much catcalling and passing of inappropriate remarks was part of the game.

At parties held in private homes, many of the games that were played in WWII are still popular today. No description is needed for Charades and Murder. In another game, guests were encouraged to break the awkward introduction stage with a simple ruse. On arrival, each guest had a sticky label attached to their back with a well-known character's name on it. The guest was expected to learn who they were supposed to be by asking the other guests a question to which the answer could only be "Yes" or "No". It was a good ice breaker to get the party going.

Another game that was particularly popular with young people was "Sardines". This was a variation of the game of hide and seek. One person was chosen to be "It" then the lights were turned down and the chosen person went off to find a hiding place somewhere in the house. The object of the game was for each of the other players to find the hiding place of the person playing "It" and to join him or her in concealment. The last person to find the communal hiding place was the loser and became the next "It".

The fun aspect of the game was the way in which everybody crammed in together in the hiding place like sardines in a can. If you were lucky you could become intimately squished in with an attractive member of the opposite sex. This game was particularly popular with the older youngsters with whom an interest in the opposite gender was an emerging drive.

Let's go to the "Flicks"

For some people, the visit to the local picture house, or cinema, was a twice-a-week event. Recognizing the popularity of this form of entertainment, the cinema managers usually changed the feature movie twice a week. For us, it involved a trip into town so our visits were less frequent. However, the movies were a major form of entertainment for everyone.

The location of the seats determined the price of the ticket. The best viewing positions commanded the highest prices but "courting couples" were content with the cheaper seats in the dark of the back rows. Privacy was hard to find for young people in the crowded conditions of British homes in those days and this was one location where it was accepted that couples should not be disturbed!

Cigarette smoking was an accepted practice in most homes and all public places. The air in the cinemas was usually thick with smoke to the extent that visibility of the screen was affected. Second hand smoke was an accepted hazard in society with little thought for its long-term effects on health.

It was usual for the film program to include a short cartoon movie, a 'Movietone' newsreel of the latest Allied victories from various war zones, and then a double bill of a B movie followed by the feature presentation. The whole program lasted as much as three hours.

The evening performances in the larger cinemas were sometimes preceded by a musician seated at a floodlit theatre organ rising from beneath the stage in front of the screen. Amid flashing coloured lights, the organist played popular songs while the words of the songs were displayed on the movie screen. A bouncing ball of light helped the audience keep time with the lyrics. The audience joined in for a full-scale sing-along of mostly jingoistic or humorous songs to set the mood for the ensuing entertainment.

Saturday mornings at the cinema were dedicated to children's programs with the price of admission reduced to be within reach of most homes. This custom was appreciated by parents as a good way to get the children out of the home for a bit of peace and quiet. There was never any peace and quiet in the cinemas on those occasions as the somewhat out-of-control audience of rowdy kids let loose all their inhibitions as they watched Mickey Mouse, Popeye, and the Roadrunner on the screen.

We made the most of it

There was no shortage of ways in which young people could have fun. Entertainment differed significantly in two ways from today's forms of relaxation. It relied on the initiative and ingenuity of the youngsters. Entertainment was not pre-packaged for them-- the ideas and fun came from within the group. Any group of young folk finding themselves together would soon come up with an informal way to pass the time. It could be as simple as playing soccer with a tennis ball or a quick game of hide-and-seek.

Secondly, nearly all of the activities took place with others. In many ways, one of the positive by-products of the war was that it created a heightened sense of community. This was true for all, including young people. It was a time when the solitary distractions of digital devices had yet to be invented. Sports equipment was less available and organized activities had to take second place behind the more important demands of the war. Young people had to depend upon their own ingenuity in order to have fun.

And this they did in spades.

Rabbits

When I look in the mirror today, I don't think my ears have grown pointy. Maybe a little furry. I do like to eat raw carrots and I can wrinkle my nose when I try hard. Despite this, I do not believe that my steady diet of eating rabbits during the formative years of ages 6 to 13 during the war has affected me physically.

On the other hand, I *was* a pretty good runner at school: I won the school cross country race one year and I was first across the line in the quarter mile in the 15 and under age group in an acceptably fast time, so maybe I should give some credit to all those rabbits that kept us well fed during WWII.

The rabbits were often on the menu at home, cooked every way my mother could devise. Rabbits baked in a pie was excellent both hot and cold. The jelly that formed in the cold version was especially good. A fricassee of tender young rabbit served with new potatoes and peas was always popular on our dining table. The taste of rabbit is mild like chicken and can be served in much the same way.

The English countryside and climate is well suited to the proliferation of all manner of edible animals. In peace time, the shooting of wild game was considered a sport and as a secondary benefit, put food on the table. In war time, the motives were

113

reversed. Food was uppermost in most people's mind and few had a chance to enjoy the sport side of the equation.

Rabbits, pigeons, pheasants, wild ducks and many other creatures suddenly became competitors for the same food that people ate, such as wheat and ripe vegetables. These animals were downgraded to the category of vermin. Even the pheasant, the rich man's favourite sport target, became a consumer of much needed grain and, consequently, a problem.

As a result, my family was allowed to purchase ammunition for our shotguns and a .22 calibre rifle. Such firearms are to be found on most farms for the control of vermin and for sport. Like most other controlled items, the shotgun ammunition came in the wartime utility format and was made available in limited quantities. Gone were the shiny red shells and the range of different shot sizes. Instead, the government-issue shells came in khaki, the colour of war, and in a limited range of shot size. Every empty shell was to be picked up after discharge and returned for refilling. This was a practice born out of economy during the war but continued in the post-war years for re-cycling and to keep the countryside free of litter.

With the population putting all their exertions into the war effort, the wildlife had a holiday from the usual number of gun-toting sportsmen roaming the countryside. Left alone from harassment, the wild creatures did the natural thing and multiplied. Edible wild game became plentiful and much in demand as a food source but difficult for the average person to obtain.

Poaching was one way in which someone could take home a couple of rabbits for the pot. Since guns were not available to most and could be heard when discharged, the knowledgeable countryman kept a ferret or two to flush the rabbits out of their holes and into waiting nets at the mouth of their burrows. This was quieter than using a gun but still required some set up and take down time in daylight when the poacher could be seen.

Wire noose snares were the quietest source of taking a rabbit or two and required little in the way of equipment. We often found such traps in the game trails weaving in and out in the hedgerows on the farm. We pulled out the anchor post and the wire noose attached to it. By the end of the war, we had dozens of snares hanging up in the barn. They were the property of the poachers but it was safe to predict that no one would come forward to claim them. The poacher could set them at night when he was not likely to be seen. The next day he would return again to pick up his victims. I regarded this as a cruel method but, when you have a family to feed, a lot of people felt this was justified. At least this was less cruel than the steel trap that usually did not kill outright and was a danger to all wild animals.

Fortunately for us, wild game was classified as vermin and thus a perfectly legal addition to our food supply. From a farmer's point of view, this was simply another harvest provided by the land.

By the age of ten, my father had schooled me in the handling of guns and safety in the field. To this day, I can still recall the tongue lashing I received when I allowed my loaded gun to point in the direction of a bystander. The gun was taken from me and I was banned from shooting for a week. I was allowed to use the .22 calibre rifle and the .410 shotgun. This was a very small gauge shotgun that could shoot a rabbit but required skill to be used against flying game birds. All my brothers had been introduced to shooting with this gun before they graduated on to the heavier weight 12 gauge shotguns.

On a quiet summer's evening, I would venture out with my .22 rifle and stalk along the hedgerows in those fields that were down to pasture. The rabbits liked to come out in the early evening light but would stay close to the safety of the hedgerows. If the bunnies heard the warning "thump, thump" sound from the rabbit on lookout duty stamping on the ground with its back foot, the whole warren would head for cover. This was a practice that Walt Disney observed, and accordingly named his cottontail character "Thumper" in the movie *Bambi*.

I would carefully pick out a young and tender adult rabbit from among the many feeding on the fresh grass. A careful stalk and I would soon be on my way home with a brace of rabbits to be hung on the game hooks in the barn. These wooden pegs in our old Elizabethan barn had been used for this same purpose for 300 years as it is the countryman's habit to hang all game for a few days before taking them into the kitchen. In cold or freezing weather, the hanging time could be as much as a week or more. All game was hung in this way to tenderize the meat just as the best cuts of beef are treated in a similar fashion today. It was the practice to hang game birds in pairs by the neck with a short length of binder twine. Rabbits and hares were first gutted and a small slit made with a knife between the tendons of one hind leg and the other leg pushed through so that the joined legs could be slipped over the wooden peg in the barn with the head hanging down.

Such was the importance of the rabbit in our culinary experience that the phrase "to skin a rabbit "came to be used to describe the process of taking off a child's sweater or jumper as it was called then. If I was the victim, my mother would say "let's skin the rabbit" and I would know to hold my arms above my head. She then held the jumper by the hem and pulled it up over my head and arms inside out. This was similar to the method used to take the skin off a rabbit by pulling it from the rear end up to the neck where the head was removed with the skin. In the ill-fitting, hand-me-down days of WWII, it felt as though my head was being removed too.

Hares are much like rabbits but are at least twice the size of their junior cousins and are a different species. They have a different lifestyle, preferring to live in open fields rather than in the woods and hedgerows. Their meat is much stronger and has a more "gamey" flavour.

There were hares on the farm but not as many as the very fertile rabbits. When we did shoot a hare, it was hung for a longer time than the rabbits and then my mother would prepare it as 'jugged hare'. Anyone who has eaten 'Civet de Lievre', as the French call it, will instantly recognize the different taste. It is a delicacy in France but does not appeal to all tastes because of its strong flavour. The meat of the hare is dark unlike the white meat of the rabbit. The cooking involves gentle simmering for a long period in a marinade of red wine, bay leaves, juniper berries and other ingredients.

The preparation of jugged hare is a dish not to be undertaken lightly and is best if accompanied by a robust red wine. Yes, a few of those French fishing boats must have been smuggling wine to Britain because it is hard to believe that the original stocks of French wine in Britain lasted right through to 1945. If you had the money or dined at one of the fancy London hotels, good French wines could still be enjoyed right through the war.

Rabbits became so plentiful in the war years that their meat became a regular feature on better restaurant menus. It was often described as chicken or some other meat possibly in French as few people regarded rabbit as a desirable dish. How wrong they were as I can attest. Many a customer must have been surprised to bite down on a piece of lead shot when he thought he was eating a farmyard chicken.

Because rabbits were not included in the meat rationing system, their flesh was also sought by butcher shops. In country towns, the local butcher often had more wild game hanging in his window than beef, pork and lamb on his counters. No questions would have been asked if a villager offered a brace of rabbits to the local butcher for a shilling or two. The poaching of rabbits, while technically illegal, was looked upon by some as a profitable form of harmless sport, whether for the home pot or for the wallet.

The demand for meat provided my family the opportunity to make some extra cash by sending the rabbits we shot to Smithfields, the wholesale meat market, on Charterhouse Street in the north-west part of London. Every two or three weeks in season, we went on safari into the fields in the early evening on a large-scale rabbit hunt. We used an old dilapidated jeep that was no longer roadworthy but could be coaxed into serving as our gun ship. The windshield could be laid flat which enabled one of us to drive while the other rode shotgun in the front passenger seat. This provided a relatively safe field of fire through 180 degrees.

As darkness descended, the rabbits came out to feed on the perimeters of the fields. Previously, we had left the gates to the fields open so that we could drive up quietly to the entrance with the headlights turned off. At the last moment, the driver roared through the gate and switched on the lights. In a five-acre field, it was not unusual to see 50 pairs of eyes reflected in the headlights. The driver quickly drove in a circle around the field while the gun bearer blazed away at the rabbits caught in the headlights. This called for quick re-loading before the rabbits recovered from their surprise and disappeared back into the safety of the hedgerows. The scene was like an episode in a Wild West movie.

With the help of Jake, Bess and Jessie, the three black Labrador gun dogs, the shot rabbits were then picked up. On a good foray, we would bag perhaps five or six rabbits in one field. Then we would move on to the next battleground and repeat the process. With up to ten suitable locations to be covered and the opportunity to go back later in the evening when the rabbits had ventured out again, we were able to mount a big score. There was one evening when we ended with a record bag of 102 rabbits by midnight.

After the rabbits had been cleaned, they were stuffed into sacks, each holding about ten rabbits. A label was attached with the name of a butcher at the Smithfields market on it and we dropped them off at the station to catch the 5:30 am. milk train to London, always the first train in the morning. It may have been early in the morning hours before the job was completed on that one occasion when we topped the record number but it was a profitable night's work. At a shilling, a rabbit we had a cheque for five pounds or so coming to us in the mail. That was the equivalent of a good week's paycheque in those days.

By dinner time that evening, diners in the Savoy Hotel and other fashionable London restaurants were munching on 'Lapin Anglais' or some such exotic sounding dish on the menu. If a diner was to lose a filling when he bit down on a lead shot, it could perhaps be called the rabbit's revenge.

Rabbits were not the only target of choice. Ring-necked wood pigeons were the scourge of farmers as they consumed a lot of grain in the summer. In the winter months when the Arctic temperatures crept down from the north, huge flocks of these birds would descend on fields of green crops and strip the plants of all leaves or at least spoil them for market. When there was a heavy freeze-up in Scandinavia, pigeons in their thousands flew over the North Sea to feed on the fields of cabbages, Brussel sprouts and kale. They were like a plague of locusts as they consumed anything green in the fields. The winter of 1940 was especially cold, and starving flocks of as many as 5,000 birds could wipe out the crop in a ten-acre field in just a week.

It was difficult to fend off an invasion of this size. Shotguns scared them off for a while but it was only a minute or so before they descended again on another part of the field. To scare them off and hope that they moved onto greener pastures elsewhere, we used what we called "banger ropes". These were lengths of natural hemp or sisal rope with small explosive gunpowder charges inserted into the strands every two inches. When the bottom of the rope was ignited the rope smoldered upwards until it set off the next charge up the rope. They created a loud bang every ten minutes or so and kept the pigeons moving. These banger ropes were also used in the cherry orchard for a similar purpose in the cherry-picking season of July.

The starving pigeons were of little use for the pot but in more nutritious times of the year we set up hides in the green crop fields and had good sport shooting the better-nourished, plumper birds. These, too, were subjected to the same treatment as the rabbits and ended up on the same milk train to London. Commuters on the later trains to London must often have wondered at the number of feathers blowing around on the platform each time we had loaded the bags of pigeons into the guard's van.

The only part of the pigeon that had enough meat on it to make it a worthwhile target was the breast. The meat is a darker colour than that of chicken and tends to be on the dry side. It was hard to pass it off as partridge, pheasant or grouse so I imagine the restaurants simply served it up as country pigeon pie with no attempt to pass it off as a more expensive dish. The problem was that many city dwellers would associate our perfectly good fresh country pigeons with the scruffy birds they saw every day leaving white droppings and feathers on the stone lions in Trafalgar Square. It was not as lucrative a market as the rabbits but the two-part return of saving the green crops and getting some money for the meat made it a worthwhile venture.

One of the great benefits of the harvesting of wildlife on the farm was that my father could supplement the relatively low wages of the farm workers with a brace of rabbits or pigeons and sometimes even a pheasant or two. A dozen eggs and an occasional free-range chicken were always welcome too. My mother's weekly session weighing babies and generally helping out at the Women's Institute clinic kept her informed of those village folks who were in need or who had suffered misfortune of some kind. I would sometimes be sent on an errand to visit a home which could use a helping hand. A knock on the door and a basket containing a couple of rabbits, a dozen eggs and some veggies was always well received.

There were other country customs that helped supplement the shortages imposed by the rationing system. In August and September, word would spread around the village that the grain in a particular field was to be cut that day. As the tractor with the reaper binder went round and round the field cutting the standing grain, the refuge for the animals got smaller and smaller. As the uncut crop diminished, some of the more athletic village members appeared on the scene armed with wooden clubs. As the sanctuary got smaller, the game taking refuge there had nowhere to go except to make a run for cover over the open stubble. To reach safety, the rabbits and other animals had to run the gauntlet of the waiting villagers. Typically less than half reached the cover of the woods.

It was always interesting to see what appeared out of the standing grain field. The majority of the animals were rabbits but other creatures would appear as well. There might be a fox or two, a mother pheasant or partridge with their youngsters that were too young to fly. These were given free passage to the safety of the hedgerows. Sometimes a household cat that had been on a hunting adventure would have to run in disgrace back to the owner's house. But it was only the rabbits that fell victim to the waiting executioners. Technically, all the rabbits that were killed belonged to the farm, but my father would gather the harvest of edible creatures together after the last cut was made and then see that everyone got something to take home for supper.

There were other customs that had been handed down through the ages. Most people kept a few laying hens in their back yard. After the grain fields had been harvested, the women and children in the village would go 'gleaning' in the fields to gather up the ears of grain that the harvest machinery had missed. It was quite common to see half a dozen women and children spread out in a line across the field bending to retrieve every last ear of wheat, oats or even the prickly ears of barley. The gleanings were then taken home to feed their chickens.

Another food source that was gleaned for the hens was a weed called 'Fat Hen' that grew wild every year on cart tracks and in the hedgerows. As the name of the weed foretells, the seed heads of this plant were much favoured by the hens. It was a favourite with the partridges and pheasants too. It was always worthwhile to send the gun dogs over to a known patch of fat hen to see if a covey of partridges was feeding there.

Mushroom hunting was a popular pastime in September and October. Although anyone foraging in the fields was really trespassing, if they were looking for edible mushrooms it was considered their traditional right to do so. To gather enough mushrooms for a good meal you had to know where the mushrooms grew every year. You also had to know which members of this fungus family were edible and which were poisonous. The difference between the appearance of a tasty field mushroom and a 'horse mushroom' or a toadstool was sometimes hard to tell. To be successful, it was necessary to set out for the fields with a hand basket and a pocket knife at an early hour. By 8:00 in the morning, the day's crop would already be in the frying pan perhaps with a slice of fried bread and a rare bit of rationed bacon. Delicious.

As well as raising chickens, many homes had a rabbit cage or two in the backyard. These rabbits were usually distinct from the wild brown ones as they came in a variety of breeds and colours from pure white to black. As a ten-year-old boy, I was always on the look-out to make a little money to add to my small allowance from my parents so I set up some rabbit cages of my own.

It might seem strange that with so many rabbits available in the wild that I would bother to create this other source. The answer was in the breed I raised. The rabbits came in a variety of colours but as a 'Rex' breed they had a particularly soft, short pelt. Their meat was good to eat and their skins could fetch a bob or two for use in clothing and gift items. At least that was the theory. Inevitably, in the typical pattern of youth, I grew tired of cleaning out the cages and despite spending hours scraping and rubbing the skins with alum to soften them for market, no buyers could be found. So much for those "get rich quick" promotions in magazines.

Eventually, I decided to leave the cage doors open and my multi-coloured, soft skinned and attractive does were a great hit with the local wild population of bucks. It wasn't long before the village residents were talking about the variety of colours the new generation of wild rabbits were wearing that year. It took two or three years before the rabbit population reverted back to its regular safe camouflage outfits. The Darwin-inspired survival of the fittest is proven once again.

Rabbits were always numerous in the English countryside but, because of the lack of control by human predators, who would be keeping their numbers in check in peace time, their population grew every year. It could be said that by 1945 there was a plague of rabbits. This created a situation in the immediate post-war years when they were susceptible to disease from overcrowding. In fact, the devastating disease myxomatosis developed, and wiped out almost all the rabbit population in Britain. There was a horrible period of a few years in which dying bunnies were wandering aimlessly throughout the woods. It was a pitiful situation. The sight of their swollen heads and the smell of their rotting bodies were so bad that few people would take their usual walks along the woodland paths.

Apparently, a doctor in France first injected the myxomatosis virus into some rabbits that were eating the vegetables in his garden. From this beginning, the disease quickly spread throughout France and across the Channel to England. It did not stop there, and it eventually spread as far away as Australia where it was welcomed by ranchers whose rabbits were so numerous they were considered a pestilence.

Rabbits are the universal prey for predators of both the human kind and other species. They helped us through the food-shortage years of WWII. The rabbit has an important role to play in the food chain. When they nearly disappeared due to myxomatosis after the war, we humans were able to switch to other food sources but the wild animal predators faced starvation. Fortunately, some rabbits developed resistance to the disease and the population made a comeback but, even 80 years later, their numbers do not match the rabbit population during WWII.

We owe a debt of thanks to rabbits for feeding us, and thereby helping win the war. They deserve a medal for the sacrifices they made just like their human partners. But wait, no. That would not be of much use to a rabbit--a medal would just gather dust in their burrows. Instead, the young people of the world came up with the perfect way to recognise the rabbits' contribution to WWII. They named a popular dance after our furry critter. Everyone was doing it. The dance was called the "Bunny Hop". This was an apt, but inadvertent, celebration of their contribution towards the winning of WWII.

The Sporting Vicar

In 1941, a German bomb landed on the houses of Parliament in London. It destroyed much of the chamber, damaged the roof structure of the clock tower, and shattered the face of Big Ben, the iconic clock rising above Parliament. Despite the damage, the chimes of Big Ben continued to ring out the hours as if in defiance against the worst the Luftwaffe could throw at the age-old city.

There were two voices that sustained the spirit of the British people during WWII. The first was of Winston Churchill, through his speeches. Who could not have been inspired by his "We will fight them on the beaches" speech after the disaster at Dunkirk? His tribute to the R.A.F. pilots in the Battle of Britain speech "Never in the history of human conflict has so much been owed by so many to so few". His "Some chicken, some neck" speech to the Canadian parliament in December 1941 with reference to the defeatist attitude of some French generals was not only memorable but helped bring the U.S. into the war. These were some of the words that sustained the resolve of the British people through the bad times in the early part of the war.

The other voice that brought reassurance to the public was the sound of the bells of Big Ben. Its deep tones spoke to the British people a message of hope and strength. The British public tuned into the nine o'clock news from the BBC every night. The broadcast was always preceded by the sound of Big Ben striking the nine o'clock hour. Not once did the famous clock fail to ring out the time throughout the war. Despite the bomb damage to the clock tower, the bells continued to ring out throughout the London blitz and to the end of the war, bringing courage and reassurance to all who heard them. The only concession to the hazards of war was the darkening of the four clock faces during the night hours. This was to make sure the illuminated dials would not serve as a navigation aid to the German bombers. The solid, deep-toned toll of the bells was a reassurance that, however much the British people were suffering, the nation was strong and would prevail.

In this digital electronic age, it is hard to appreciate that much of life throughout the British countryside measured its day by the chimes of the local church clock. Minutes were not really important as most church clocks rang out the time every fifteen minutes. If you wanted a more accurate time, you would make a judgement call as to how many minutes had passed since the last chimes. Wrist watches were rare. If someone had a fob watch and had remembered to wind it up the night before, you could be more accurate but for most matters in rural England that kind of accuracy was not important. It is true that the trains could not afford to be so lax but even there the guard with his green and red flags would take the time to see that everyone was safely onboard before blowing his whistle. The train schedule took second priority to allowing enough time for the very young, the infirm and the wounded to board without undue haste.

All this was true in our village. The church clock regularly chimed the quarter, half and full hours and could be heard over a wide area, including most of the far reaches of our farm. The farm labourers would rely on its chimes when they were working the fields. If they were with a team of draught horses, these smart animals, too, would know instinctively when it was time to "knock off". Whereas the church clock was important to us all, I cannot say that we were loyal supporters of the church. As in most parishes, it was the personality of the vicar which determined how many of his flock would turn up for Sunday services. For a brief while in the 1940's, we did have a young vicar with whom many in the village could relate. Despite a minor physical ailment which kept him out of the armed forces, he was a strong supporter of the village sports teams and showed an interest in farming and wildlife matters. He was what you might call a practical vicar. He was just like one of us. Even when he stood in the pulpit, he spoke our language and not ecclesiastical gobbledygook.

The local church dates back to the 14th century and, at one time, the village could even claim an Archbishop of Canterbury as a favourite son. St. Simon de Mepeham bore the shepherd's crook from 1328 to 1333. The records show that he was born in 1275 and died in office in 1333. There is some question as to his career because the records show that he was excommunicated (for what reason it is not stated). Nonetheless, the church claimed him as a founder.

As often is the case with old village churches, the elm trees surrounding the church and the graveyard had grown very large as the years went by. The local population of rooks and jackdaws had taken over the tops of the trees to form a large 'rookery' where they built their nests and raised their young. Rooks resemble crows in that they are all black and are about the same size, perhaps a touch smaller. Jackdaws are also black except for a grey coloured head. Jackdaws are the packrats of the bird world in that they love to collect small sparkly items and decorate their nests with them. Rooks and jackdaws are from the same order as crows but they are a different family even though they look like each other. Their numbers had swollen considerably, possibly because of the war and the lack of human intrusion in their lives from sportsmen and gamekeepers.

In normal times, the "cawing" of the nesting rooks was just a part of the environment and atmosphere of the church. However, during the nesting season every spring, the birds became particularly numerous and noisy. When the number of the birds increased to the point where the vicar's sermons were hard to hear over the cacophony of their cawing and the smell from their

droppings permeated the air around the church, the vicar came to my family to seek a solution.

There seemed to be only one answer. As farmers, my family were allowed to keep sporting guns and, more importantly, to buy ammunition for them. The permit to buy the ammunition was expressly so that we could keep down the numbers of vermin which could be a threat to the nation's food production. Rooks eat a lot of seed grain in the spring planting season so their definition as vermin was easy to justify. However, in all fairness, it should be said that rooks were excellent at eating small insects as well as the seed grain. In this way, they are probably more helpful than a hindrance to food production. Nonetheless, the vicar needed our help and we were happy to oblige.

We felt the use of 12 gauge shotguns would be too noisy and might disturb the residents living near the church. In the nesting season when the young birds have just hatched, they leave the nest and sit on the high branches of the elm trees for a day or two until they are strong enough to take the plunge and fly. At this vulnerable point in time, the ideal weapon was a .22 rifle. This is a small bore rifle that makes very little noise when fired. We had two of these guns available together with enough rounds to go with them.

We discussed the plan with the vicar and he decided it would be best to start the cull of the young rooks on a weekday early in the week. My brother John was just old enough to join the village troop of the Home Guard. He suggested this would be a good opportunity for these would-be home defence troops to practice their shooting skills. One or two of these warriors also had .22 rifles they could bring along. At the appointed hour, the Home Guard platoon paraded at the church with the vicar taking the honorary role of battle commander. The troops were given their orders and deployed throughout the graveyard.

Gravestones always had the distinction among country-folk of being excellent grindstones for the sharpening of knives, scythes and other cutting tools used in rural life. Granite headstones, being the hardest, were most likely the best for sharpening a dull blade. The finishing touch for the final edge was probably achieved by switching to the limestone or some other softer stone. Country folk are nothing if not practical and for a relative who has passed on to be of continued service after his allotted time would likely be considered natural. It would likely draw a comment of appreciation in the local pub of an evening. Practical as the headstones are for the good husbandry of the land, the use of these same stones as convenient rests for sharpshooters was pushing their usefulness to the limit. Nonetheless, when the members of the Home Guard saw the vicar taking up his position with a .22 rifle propped on the top of a headstone it was a signal that it was OK to follow suit. The words "Rest in Peace" carved below the trigger guard of a rifle seemed in striking contrast with the real wishes of those who had commissioned the farewell message.

The cull commenced and black bodies fell to the ground. Distraught adult rooks took off with much clamour and circled high overhead in a distraught flock. There was little the young birds could do to avoid their fate as they had yet to learn how to fly. When sufficient numbers had been shot, a whistle was blown and the sound of rifle shots ceased. The first and only battle action that was required of the local army of villagers was over. The clean-up of the carnage commenced and soon there were three or four sacks of black birds waiting for disposal. With the return to relative calm, the flock of adult rooks circling like a black storm cloud overhead began their descent to the tops of the elm trees. Much cawing and bird chatter continued as the parents assessed the situation. It wasn't long before the rooks and jackdaws settled down and resumed their family duties. It was almost as if they took this interruption to their daily lives as just another necessary procedure and the answer was to return to the nest and lay more eggs to replace the missing family members. Could it be that other forms of life can handle catastrophes better than humans? For the birds, it was just another unfortunate step in the cycle of life and death. For the assailants on both sides of the human conflict, such a philosophical acceptance was not possible as the war of attrition continued on.

In the meantime, it seemed a shame that the fresh meat of the young rooks should go to waste, especially with the meat ration at its lowest ebb. Much speculation followed as to how the war effort could be helped by the proper use of this good protein. Rooks are very little different physically from pigeons, partridges and other wild gamebirds commanding good prices in the butcher shops. There is not a lot of meat on any of these birds except in the breast meat. Even so, few if any of 'Dad's Army' members, as the Home Guard was affectionately known, fancied taking full advantage of their victims. "If it was served to you as breast of chicken, pigeon or even pheasant in a restaurant, you wouldn't know the difference", said some of the members. "Well, I don't know…I just don't fancy eating rook" was the general feeling.

"Wait a minute," said one of the riflemen, turning to my brother, "I know you've been sending rabbits and pigeons up to Smithfields market on the milk train in the mornings, why not do the same with these. Let the butchers in London decide what to do with the fresh meat." It was decided. The sacks of birds were tied shut at the top and the labels supplied by the Smithfield butcher were attached. No mention was made of the species of bird within the sacks. That was left for the butcher to decide and to dispose of as he thought fit.

By five thirty the next morning, the sacks were on the station platform waiting to be loaded into the guard's van with the milk cans from various dairy farms down the line. We didn't have to wait long before the cheque arrived in the mail.

The next Sunday the church was unusually full. The vicar's sermon could be heard all the way to the back pews. He announced appreciation for a mysterious and generous donation to the church fund for feeding the poor. No mention was made as to who was the donor despite the knowing looks passed between the Home Guard members. The rooks and the jackdaws in the elm trees could be seen back on their nests. In London, the diners at the posh Savoy Hotel were feeling comfortable after an excellent Sunday lunch of game pie in the Savoy Grill.

Upon reflection, it may be that we were not the first to offer these black feathered birds as a source of good nutrition to people in high places. You have only to cast your mind back to traditional English nursery rhymes to find a similar situation.

If you check the words of the 18th century nursery rhyme "Sing a song of sixpence", the words will have a familiar ring. Just to remind you, here is an extract from the lyrics:

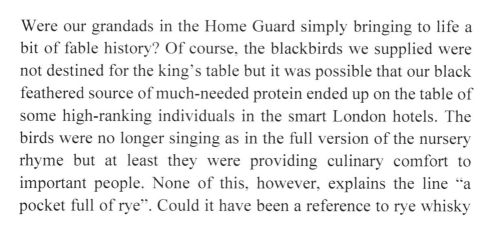

Sing a song of sixpence, a pocket full of rye
Four and twenty black birds baked in a pie
...
Wasn't that a dainty dish to set before a king

Were our grandads in the Home Guard simply bringing to life a bit of fable history? Of course, the blackbirds we supplied were not destined for the king's table but it was possible that our black feathered source of much-needed protein ended up on the table of some high-ranking individuals in the smart London hotels. The birds were no longer singing as in the full version of the nursery rhyme but at least they were providing culinary comfort to important people. None of this, however, explains the line "a pocket full of rye". Could it have been a reference to rye whisky or beer? Hardly suitable for a children's nursery rhyme. Perhaps the pocket full of rye was destined for something as nutritional as a loaf of rye bread for the child's grandad! No doubt the Home Guard members would have welcomed the former interpretation.

The posters on the billboards urged us to "Waste Not, Want Not". The vicar and his troops had done as requested. The resonate peals of Big Ben continued to reassure Londoners and with the passage of time the fortunes of war began inexorably to turn in Britain's favour.

The Farm as Provider

I am not sure whether it should be called sharing our good fortune, breaking the law or just doing what's right. As a source of food in a time when food was rationed, it was important for the farm to be seen to be contributing to the war effort rather than taking advantage of the opportunities presented in a time of shortages. It was a fine balance.

There is no doubt we were fortunate to be living on the farm. We were never short of food of one kind or another. At times, we were eating a steady diet of what was available and not necessarily what we would have liked but that was a small price to pay. If we were ever short of meat, it was easy to go out and shoot a couple of rabbits for the pot, except in the spring when it was a golden rule at home that you leave the wildlife alone in the breeding season. Not that rabbits have much of what you might call a breeding season as they seem to be at it all year long.

Vegetables were available at most times throughout the year either from the garden or from the farm fields. Even in the frozen days of January and February there were cabbages and Brussels sprouts in the fields. These were frost resistant and bags of them were sent to London every day by the milk train early in the morning. They were delivered to Covent Garden Market where an agent handled them and sent us a weekly cheque.

When the farm grew potatoes, they were stored on the sides of the fields in what we called 'clamps'. The potatoes were piled up in rows about three feet high and then covered in straw with a thick covering of earth. This was enough to keep them from freezing and the clamp could be opened at one end, the potatoes removed as needed and the clamp sealed again. The potatoes, too, were sent to Coventry Garden.

There was always a flock of chickens running free around the farmyard. They produced absolutely the tastiest eggs as they picked up the spilled grain, ate the fresh grass and foraged for all manner of insects. In winter, they were fed a hot mash of kitchen leftovers with a little flour added. This was the same diet that was fed to the three Labrador gun dogs Jake, Bess and Jessie, my father's favourite Border Collie sheep dog and Pepper, our Fox Terrier, whose job it was to keep down the population of mice and rats. For the dogs, there was usually some left over bones of one kind or another added to their mash. There was never any need for special chicken or dog food. Living on a farm, you learned how to utilize everything that you had and to be almost self-sufficient.

This same principle applied to the bees. My mother tended three or four hives of bees which were kept in the cherry orchard. Since we were known to keep bees, there was always great excitement when someone from the village phoned to say they had spotted a swarm of bees that had flown from a hive with a newly hatched queen bee and settled in a tree somewhere. This was an opportunity to add a new hive to our apiary. We would rush off to the location of the swarm with a smoker device and a cardboard box in which to bring home the amazing sight of hundreds or perhaps thousands of bees clinging to each other with the eloping queen out of sight in the middle of this humming mass.

Quite unafraid, my mother would don her old hat with the mesh screen hanging around her head and shoulders and quietly talk to the bees as she puffed smoke around them from the smoldering cardboard in the smoker. As the smoke caused them to calm down one of us cut the branch to which they were clinging and gently lowered the pulsating mass of bees into the cardboard box. A few extra puffs as we drove back home kept them quiet until we could introduce them to their new home of a hastily assembled hive for the new tenants.

Bees were needed to pollinate the blossoms of the cherry trees and the few apple and plum trees growing in the orchard. A by-product of this valuable function was that the bees produced excellent honey. If you take the honey out of the hive, you must substitute sugar for their food so that the bees will survive the cold winter when they hibernate in the hive huddled together to keep warm. I was always amazed how warm it was inside a hive even on the coldest days.

During the war, the government recognized the need to keep bees active and healthy so we were allowed a special ration of sugar for them. At various times during the war, the country ran short of sugar and rations were cut. My beekeeping mother juggled the supply of honey with the availability of sugar.

Sometimes we ate the sugar assigned to the bees and left them the honey. When the reverse was true and the ration of sugar was adequate, we took the honey and gave them the sugar. This made a lot of sense to us but I wonder if the bureaucrats in the Ministry of Food would have considered this in contravention of some food rationing act. But that's how you managed in wartime: you did what you had to do, finding a way to circumvent the minor rules while respecting the more important ones.

As a result of the sugar shortages, the jam availability was always a problem. On most school holidays, my eldest brother John would bring home two or three fellow students from school. The idea was that they would work on the farm to earn a little money and do their bit for the war effort. Farm workers were hard to get due to the conscription of younger men into the armed forces. The students were usually in the 15 to 17 age range as the call-up age was 18. With their young age and the hard, physical work, their appetites were huge and my mother had to devise a rationing system at the dinner table. Most foods were available in adequate supply but the jams and butter would disappear overnight if not rationed out. On the table at mealtimes, there would be half a dozen jam jars and butter bowls each with the owner's name on it. To be fair, family members were subjected to the same treatment while the students were with us.

We provided the board and lodging and paid them a small wage. Every bedroom in the house was brought into use. Fortunately, it was a large old house with three floors. We had to clean up the attic to make an additional two bedrooms. The attic was a spooky place with piles of old Victorian bric-a-brac stored there in those 19th century round-topped steamer trunks. It was a fabulous source for dress-up clothes and old military memorabilia. There was even a vintage 8 mm hand-cranked movie projector with a supply of Charlie Chaplin silent movies. The movies were on highly flammable film that had to be cranked at just the right speed. If you were too slow, a circle would appear in the centre of the screen and rapidly spread until the film burned right through. The heat of the projection bulb was too hot for the delicate film strip. We were forever splicing the burned film together and the movies got shorter and shorter.

It was hard work for the students, especially for those not used to country ways. We would start out with perhaps three boarders but we could predict that we would soon be down to only two. After three or four days of hard work in the fields, we could anticipate a telegram or a phone call for one of them announcing that somebody was not well in their family and would they please come home. We knew that this was a set-up arranged by the student who didn't like the hard work. After they had gone, there were knowing chuckles all round as it was so predictable. And understandable, too, as it was hard work for what were often city boys with no experience of physical labour.

There was one fellow though who came several years in a row. His name was Mike Braachi. He was as strong as an ox. He was a bit of a brain and went on to university and made a name for himself in the scientific world after the war. In order to pay for his expenses prior to his university studies, I understand he signed on to a whaling ship for a six-month tour. This was a particularly hard job. At the time, I thought that sounded like an exciting venture which I would have liked to do as they set off for the Antarctic but I learned later that it was pure drudgery in awful conditions and really very cruel. But I suppose the money was good.

Thanks to the bees, we usually had a good crop of cherries. While I was away at school, we would eagerly await the arrival of four or five cake tins filled with ripe cherries that were a treat for the whole school of 80 or more boys. Even in war time, the Post Office delivery was fast. The packaged tins of cherries usually arrived within two days of being mailed. However, since they arrived in the heat of summer we wasted no time in eating them. In comparison to school food, this was a welcome treat.

My father never raised milk cows or pigs: beef cattle, sheep, grain crops, and market garden vegetables but never either of these two high labour-intensive animals. They required a special method of farming which my father decided not to undertake. We used to tease him that he didn't like to get up early in the morning to milk cows and didn't like the smell of pigs. In fact, he was usually up earlier than any of us but the farm buildings were not set up for either of these two types of farming and too many irons in the fire, so to speak, can often be inefficient.

Raising sheep is a demanding occupation, especially in the lambing season of March and April. Luckily, we had an experienced shepherd whose sole job it was to care for the sheep. In lambing season, the shepherd's hut was wheeled into the lambing pens and Ted, the shepherd, lived and slept in that hut with very few breaks until the lambing was over. We would supply him with hot meals and he would sleep on a pile of sheepskins in the hut often accompanied by two or three lambs which had been rejected by the ewes or whose mother had died. If a lamb died at birth, Ted would take the skin off the dead lamb and tie it onto the back of a lamb whose mother had died and therefore needed a foster mother. The surrogate mother would likely accept the orphaned lamb so long as the substitute lamb smelled like the one to which she had given birth.

If the shepherd could not get other ewes to adopt the orphan lambs, we would take them back to the farmhouse for bottle feeding and warmth. This was the responsibility of we younger children and we loved doing it. It was not unusual to be greeted at the door by a lamb bleating for its mother or after bonding with us looking for human company and a nice warm bottle of milk. As children, we would enjoy feeding them from a wine bottle with a rubber teat fitted over the neck. It was surprising how strong they were as they constantly thrust their lips forward to force the milk through the teat. They had no teeth at that stage so when we first taught them how to take the milk, we would put some milk on our fingers and they would suck them with great enthusiasm. To keep warm they spent the nights snuggled in blankets in a box by the kitchen fire. During the lambing season, our order with the milkman would be increased by two or three pints each day.

After a few days, the lambs would be big enough to rejoin the flock and we would be sad to see them go. By then, they would have been given names and the bond was hard to break for both parties. If, at some later stage, a full-grown lamb was selected to be taken behind the barn and slaughtered, we would wonder if this had been one of the lambs we had helped to raise a few months earlier.

Farm life is nothing if not practical and matters such as this were taken in stride. We were aware that slaughtering on the farm for private use of the meat was against the law but who was to say that this lamb had not been a victim of enemy action or a falling piece of our own anti-aircraft shells. Besides, it was only on rare occasions that we killed our own sheep. If we did so, it was usually in preparation for a wedding or some other festivity in the village and the celebrants were unlikely to raise the issue, assuming they even knew of the source of the fine meal. Yes, you had to be practical in wartime and the bending of the odd rule for the benefit of all made good sense.

With the above exception, all of our livestock, when ready for market, was sent to the Tuesday market in nearby Rochester. Here the cattle and sheep were bought by the local butchers and taken for slaughter elsewhere. Our local butcher, Mr. King, had a shop half a mile down the road. When we had a particularly good load of cattle going to market, my father would let Mr. King know and he would buy a nice fat steer from that load. We would not be able to buy any more of the meat than our ration cards would allow but we knew we were getting good quality and we knew there would be no thumb on the weigh scale when our ration was cut.

Since the farm did not have any dairy cattle, we did not have access to butter and milk. Milk was not a problem as the daily delivery of our milk ration was substantial enough. It was left each day at our side door where it was important to bring it into the house before the birds got to it first. The small birds known as Blue Tits and the slightly larger Great Tits seemed particularly fond of the cream on the top of the bottle. They would peck off the thin cardboard tops and help themselves. They got to know the time when the milkman came by and could be seen waiting in the nearby bushes ready to take their breakfast drink as soon as he left.

Butter was in very short supply and the ration coupons at one low point allowed us only 2 oz. per person per week but we had a solution for that. The Bolster farm at the south end of the village kept a few cows and made their own butter. It was what you might call 'country style' butter churned by hand and with an intense flavour. It was very yellow and tasted like a cross between cheese and butter. It was not to everyone's taste but when our ration of the more anaemic national brand ran out, we were happy to switch to its strong taste.

Since we had plenty of eggs from our own hens and the Bolster farm did not have chickens, there was a natural opportunity for a straight swap. Once every week or so, our farm car would make the two-mile journey and drive round to the back door of the dairy farm. A quick knock on the door and two packages would be traded. No conversation, just a rapid exchange and straight home again. Was this legal? Probably not, but little harm was done as the butter and eggs were just from small producers and not part of the national supply of butter and eggs through the Ministry of Food sources.

The eggs the farm raised were mostly from chickens but there were usually a few geese running free in the farmyard, bullying every living thing, including the dogs. They were afraid of no one and could land a nasty peck on any person or animal they didn't like. If we felt like a goose egg for breakfast, the potential diner was told to go and get it from the goose himself. This was a hazardous process requiring subterfuge and the assistance of a partner whose job was to distract the goose away from the nest. A quick run in and grab tactic usually worked but woe betide you if the goose realized what was happening.

My mother was in charge of the chicken flock and the geese came under her jurisdiction too. She was perfectly happy selecting a couple of young cockerels for the Sunday lunch and quite nonchalant about ringing their necks. Holding them upside down in her left hand she would grab their necks with her right hand. A quick snap downwards and the execution was over in a flash. She would bring the dead but still flapping birds in from the chicken run without giving it much thought.

When it came to killing two geese for Christmas, it was a different procedure altogether. The ferocity of the geese did not faze her but the breaking of their necks did present a problem as they were very strong. We finally resolved the matter with my mother holding a flapping goose upside down by the legs with her two hands while two of us put a broom handle over the neck of the goose on the ground and stood on each end of the handle. My mother gave a quick yank upwards, its neck was broken and the goose dead. It was all in the day's work for a lady who raised seven children and was in charge of feeding a family of nine plus the waifs and strays that we would often bring home. She was one of those persons who just believed that whatever the need, you just got on with it with a minimum of fuss. Two more for dinner tonight? No problem. Just set two more places at the table and two more baking potatoes in the oven.

Realizing that living on the farm was seen by many less fortunate people as an advantage that could create a sense of envy and jealousy, my parents went out of their way to be generous to those in need. My mother helped out regularly at a weekly clinic run by the local Women's Institute. The clinic was there to provide a service to young mothers, older folk, and those wives and mothers anxious about their menfolk serving overseas and in dangerous circumstances. In addition to the help she could provide in the clinic, she was able to pick up information about those people in the village who could benefit from some of the extra food we could offer. There were many occasions when I was dispatched with a couple of chickens, a box of cherries or a dozen eggs to a home in the village to help out someone going through a rough patch.

The airmen manning the three balloon sites on the farm always welcomed a basket of goodies or perhaps a hot cooked stew to add to their basic rations. The airmen in the balloon site in the meadow beside the house were doubly pleased when one of

My mother, who made it all happen

my sisters made the delivery. Their site overlooked the back garden of the farmhouse and much of their work involved just sitting around watching the balloon. They preferred to watch in the direction of our house in the hope that one of my sisters would appear and hang out the washing on the clothesline or perform some other chore which eased their monastic existence.

Because we had spare living space and because we could provide a good diet, we were asked by the authorities to take in some repatriated Allied prisoners of war. On several occasions, we had some very thin servicemen boarded with us for a month or two of recuperative leave. These ex-POWs were usually from a Commonwealth country since they could not go back to their homes to recover. I remember two South Africans, thin as rakes, who spent their time with us exercising in the garden, sleeping a lot, and eating well. They had been rescued from a German POW camp in the later stages of the war.

There was always more than enough exercise for our family members just doing the chores on the farm. I was fascinated to see these two POW's going through prescribed athletic exercises on the lawn trying to hasten their recovery. To me, it seemed more sensible that they should get their exercise by helping with the chores or playing lawn cricket with me. The concept of formal exercise was foreign to me at that age.

Often, I was not sure who would be coming down to breakfast each morning. We had a constant flow of friends of the family on a couple of days leave and nowhere to spend it. There were one or two young cousins we cared for over an extended period of time for whatever reason. We had the facilities so my parents welcomed them without hesitation. The house was always full of people whether family or not.

These were just a few of the many people that benefitted from what the farm could offer.

My parents accepted that we were more fortunate than many and recognized that this good fortune came with responsibilities. With the hard work and generosity that they provided for the many people they helped, they more than compensated for their favourable circumstances. They were some of the numerous civilians who "did their bit" in WWII.

As for me, as a young boy I never really appreciated the gravity of the war years. I was able to enjoy the excitement of the times without realizing how very difficult it was for so many people. Maybe that was just as well as war should never involve children. For my safe and exciting wartime experiences, I shall be forever grateful for the sacrifices of others.

Hand-me-downs Brought Me Up

For the first few weeks of the war, most goods in the shops were still available but customers soon found they were only to be had in smaller quantities at the discretion of the shopkeeper. Some items were kept 'under the counter' for regular customers. The retailer would open packages and divide up the contents into smaller units for sale. For instance, my father was able to purchase only one or two razor blades at a time when the original package contained six.

This was a form of rationing imposed by the shopkeeper in an attempt to favour regular customers and to make goods in short supply available to more people. As more and more factories were switched over from the production of consumer goods to essential war material, some items became unavailable for the duration of the war.

Eventually, inventories of items no longer produced ran out and second-hand sales became the only way to obtain such goods. A black market existed in which most luxury goods could be obtained. But for most people this was a world in which they chose not to dabble.

Factories continued to manufacture clothing and shoes but precious ration coupons were required for these. The range of clothing styles was limited and fell under the category of 'utility' garments. In other words, they were basic, dull, limited in choice and with little sense of style.

To support this concept, Winston Churchill was seen regularly in his unflattering 'siren suit' as an example to us all that practical clothing was not only OK but was a statement of national support for our servicemen.

For my school uniform, I required a jacket with the school crest on the breast pocket, the school tie and a cap in the school colours. After initial stocks of new uniform pieces ran out at the officially appointed shops, there was only one source for these items--from students who had outgrown them or left school. Every year the school would organize a jumble sale at which these garments would find a new home until finally they became so threadbare that they were given to the rag and bone man as he toured the residential streets.

Since I had three brothers who had passed through the school system ahead of me I was inevitably the recipient of their outgrown school uniforms and other clothing. In most cases, they had attended the same schools so their clothing was held in anticipation of my finally growing big enough to fit into their cast-offs. In a few cases, the school jackets were not second hand but third hand or had come from even more previous owners.

In this respect, I was no different from most of my classmates. We all faced the same shortages and, to tell the truth, we didn't really mind what we looked like as ten-year-olds. We judged each other more in terms of our sports abilities, our physical strengths, the extent of our shrapnel collections, and possibly whether or not we qualified as a 'brain' at school work. And, if I am honest, I admit we also reflected our relative social standing in the rampant class structure of the era.

Bicycles were an important part of our social life. Although we had two cars on the farm, they were for official farm business. In the early stages of the war, a very small petrol ration was made available to car owners, however, with so many fathers away in the armed forces and the petrol allowance being so small, most families that possessed cars put them up on blocks for the duration.

We had a special allocation of petrol for farm use in the tractors but it contained a red dye in it so that the police would know if it was being used for personal driving. Red coloured petrol in the farm tractors was fine but we had to be very careful what coloured petrol was in the tanks of the Hillman Minx and the Austin. If they were on official farm business it was OK but if we were in the back seats with buckets and spades and a picnic basket for the beach, the consequences would have been severe. For the most part, we obeyed the rules on this point. Mind you, an occasional visit to one of the small sections of beaches which had not been closed by mines may have been undertaken with a slight tinge of colour in the fuel.

Because of the shortage of petrol for all purposes, there were not many cars on the roads. Our usual means of transportation was the bicycle. As far as I was concerned, this meant a hand-me-down bike. With so many siblings ahead of me, there was always one left over in my size as we all grew up in age and dimensions.

My first wheeled transportation was a well-used tricycle. I was the seventh and last owner as I believe it was scrapped after I graduated to a two-wheeler. It deserved its final rest after serving all seven of us in the family. When I inherited it, there were already signs of age and misuse and it even had a slightly buckled rear wheel. Nonetheless, it was my passport to freedom. It took me to Miss Wheelan's kindergarten school every day and on other outings around the village.

With a doubled-up cigarette card attached to the frame so that the turning rear wheel snapped it every time a spoke flicked by, it made a sound like an engine. At least that is how it sounded to my young imaginative mind. To me, it was an armoured tank or Spitfire and I was the pilot shooting down Messerschmitt 109s. I know I was a drag on any trips with my older brothers on their bikes as a tricycle has no gears and requires a lot of effort to peddle on even the slightest inclines. But as I grew bigger, I inherited their bikes and was soon flying down the hills with the best of them.

Jumble sales were very popular. They were somewhere you went to pick up some bargains, usually clothing, but also toys and other household items. The village hall was a favourite venue for these well-attended events. Jumble sales were also the place where housewives could meet and discuss the latest events. The portable upright mirror in the corner constantly had a line-up of half-clad ladies checking out the suitability of potential fashion finds. I don't believe any men would have dared to enter the village hall when a sale was on. They would have been frog-marched off the premises and accused of being Peeping Toms.

Popular items at such events were discarded parachutes. These were made of a fabric that felt like silk and were therefore much in demand for cutting up and sewing into ladies underwear. Little did that German pilot floating down from the sky realize that he was bringing such a fine gift to the ladies of Britain.

Sometimes, panels of nylon printed with road maps of France, Holland and Germany were available. They were part of the equipment taken by airmen when they flew over occupied Europe. These were maps printed on fabric that would survive a wet or rough landing better than the usual paper maps. They were designed to help downed aircrew find their way to safety. Their secondary use was soon discovered to be for home sewing into scarves and other garments. Since they were printed in colour they were much in demand in a fashion world bored with the drab tones of the utility brand of government-approved clothing.

Until the American troops arrived, silk or nylon stockings were almost unattainable so the ladies faked the appearance of stockings by carefully drawing a line up the rear of their calves. When the GI's appeared on the scene in 1943, the first stop they made before going off base was to the PX store where they loaded up with silk stockings and chocolate bars. This ensured their welcome among the women and children but earned them the antagonism of the men. The slogans 'Welcome, GI's' and 'Go Home, Yanks' had a decidedly gender bias.

On one occasion, I was in complete disgrace because in a misguided attempt to be helpful I placed my mother's new shoes too near the kitchen fire in an attempt to dry them out after she had been caught in a heavy rain storm. They were there for too long and too near the flames with the result that the poor-quality leather (or perhaps fake leather) dried out and cracked. Precious clothing coupons had been used to purchase those shoes and it would be some months before enough coupons would be available again in a new ration card.

Another time, my sister had found a lovely pre-war style jacket in one of the London shops. On the evening train ride, home she fell asleep and, in her hurry to wake up and get off at her station, she left the package in the overhead rack on the train. The Lost and Found services of the Southern Railway were practically non-existent and that jacket graced somebody else's shoulders at the expense of my sister's clothing coupons. A major tragedy on the home front.

A similar disaster happened to my brother, John. Working in all weathers on the farm, he needed a good waterproof coat. The waxed surface on his old rain proof jacket had dried out and cracked. Since a new waterproof was out of the question, he decided to recondition the leaky one. For this he placed some linseed oil in a ten-gallon drum and immersed the coat in the oil. In the orchard behind the house was a clothesline where the washing was hung out to dry and a fire pit where garbage was burned off. John placed the drum on the smouldering ashes in the fire pit and threw on a few extra pieces of firewood. The oil heated up nicely and began to soak into the fabric of the coat. At this point a spark from the fire landed in the drum igniting the hot oil with a huge blast of flame and a loud explosion.

The airmen in the nearby barrage balloon camp had been gazing through their binoculars to see if it was my sister Pat who had come out to the clothesline as she was a favourite with the boys in the camp. When the airmen saw the huge flame, they went rushing down with a fire extinguisher to save her only to be disappointed to find brother John with a blackened face and no trace of his old waterproof coat. For their 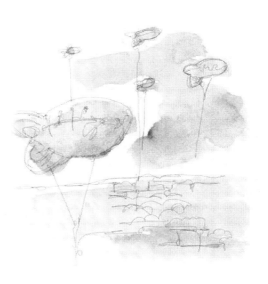 good intentions, my mother baked a cake and Pat delivered it to them the next day.

In truth, we were very happy to have these four airmen camped so close to the house. They were nice guys and were helpful in many ways on several occasions. They had a lot of downtime while babysitting their balloon and were only too happy to lend a hand around the farm when the need arose.

Christmas time was an occasion which stretched the imagination to come up with suitable presents. Great ingenuity was required to find gifts that were something more than just what people needed. There wasn't much to buy in the shops so we had to turn to our own resources to provide the answers. This in turn required careful thought and planning. The rule of thumb in the family was that each person got one major gift in the Christmas stocking and one little fun item from the tub decorated as a snowman on the table at tea time.

I remember saying that I liked the socks that I had seen on a clown at a children's party. They were all the colours of the rainbow. That Christmas I got what I wished for: a pair of socks hand knitted with all the left over coloured wools from my mother's knitting box. The first day I wore them I was ridiculed with laughter by my friends and those socks never saw the light of day again.

Our teachers were helpful in coming up with ideas for Christmas gifts for our families. When November rolled around, our art classes concentrated on fabricating gifts from odds and ends we could find. Christmas cards made by carving a potato in such a way that it could be used like a rubber stamp to stencil pictures of holly, snowflakes, bells and other symbols were standard items. Unusual bits of driftwood sanded and polished made good paperweights for fathers. Old cigar boxes or any boxes of a similar shape were painted and covered with floral decals.

They were given to mothers as boxes in which to store their odds and ends. Chicken eggs with the yolk and white carefully blown out to make an omelette were then painted to become Christmas tree decorations.

For best friends in our boy's gang, we would take an old toothpaste carton, add a couple of wings, a tail and lots of camouflage paint to create our rendition of a Spitfire. For some reason, Balsa wood kits to make airplane gliders remained in good supply well into the war years. These were always popular with the 8 to 12 age group. If you were really lucky, you could still find the kits with a propeller and an elastic band which could be wound up and launched for some long loop-the-loop flights of these light weight but fragile toys.

Of course, weapons had a fascination for us boys. Catapults, or slingshots, were always needed as the home-made versions had a limited lifespan. A visit to the woods with a saw provided the necessary forked stick. That was the easy part. Wheedling an old car inner tube from the local garage wasn't too difficult especially as one tube could provide the elastic strips for 20 catapults. Attaching the rubber strips to the ends of the Y forks of the stick needed skill and very careful binding with strong thread. Ammunition was as easy as just keeping a sharp eye out for the right sized pebbles. After that, it was just a matter of perfecting one's skill, shooting those pebbles with some degree of accuracy.

Most boys had their pretend gun. We didn't bother with making replicas of pistols because all you had to do was to hold out your right hand with the index and forefingers pointed while the thumb held the other two fingers folded under it. In our cops and robbers games or our Germans versus Brits games, all you had to do was to point your hand gun at the enemy and shout "Tschoo, tschoo--you're dead!" Or if you had no imagination, simply "bang, bang--you're dead!" would suffice.

Rifles and machine guns provided more opportunity for originality. An old broom handle for the barrel with a triangular piece of wood nailed on at one end for the butt provided the right shape. Following that, a nail on the end of the barrel provided the foresight and another nail at the front of the butt became the trigger. Add some pursed lips and more spit-inducing "tschoo, tschoo"ing and you were a fully-armed soldier. This was all you needed to join in any war battle or "Capture the Flag" games. Naturally, many of us took our weapons to a higher level of authenticity with some impressive examples of hand carved rifles. A good replica of a rifle definitely provided status in the games we played and the commanders on each side were usually chosen by the reality of their weapons.

It is hard to imagine but ten-year-old boys were seen knitting wool squares on their mothers' knitting needles. The plan was for these squares to measure 6 inches each way and for the finished squares to be sewn later into blankets for wounded soldiers and those in need. My squares tended to be more like 7 inches by 5 inches as my stitches got tighter and tighter. However, it was the thought that counted and I imagine some poor fellow was happy to have a shawl or blanket of any size and shape to keep him warm on those cold winter nights.

Perhaps the greatest indication of the shortage of everyday items was the need to use and re-use paper. Nice clean sheets of writing paper were soon a thing of the past. Letters from the authorities were printed on a flimsy buff paper made from recycled, previously used stock.

This was wholly appropriate as every economy was needed to keep "our boys" fighting in the front lines. Notably, the headmaster of my school went one step further when he suggested we should save all envelopes and cut them down one side and at the end to be flattened out so that the insides could be used for our school work. In fact, I think school notebooks were available but he wanted to make a statement about the need for us all to contribute to the war effort.

Our headmaster was like that. A traditional old warrior from WWI frustrated that he was too old to serve in the armed services in this war. Not a bad chap.

Work and Play

As far as possible, the school authorities tried to keep sports programs and other recreational activities continuing as though the war did not exist. There were fewer young teachers around so some of the retirees were enrolled to take their places in coaching and supervising games. There were some restrictions as far as the availability of equipment was concerned and travel between different sports teams for home and away games was not always possible. Nonetheless, the school authorities tried to keep our activities continuing with as little disruption as possible.

The cricket field could be spotted with white-clad players one minute, the next minute there would be a rush for shelter as the wail of the air raid siren was heard. The batsman would complain that he was about to make his best batting score ever, the bored fielder in long leg position would say, "Good old Adolf, saved from a boring game I am forced to play. Now where did I leave my Beano comic?" But on the whole, life on the playing fields continued much as before.

Home and Away matches are an integral part of a school's sports program. Travel restrictions and the availability of fuel to drive the teams to other schools confined the radius of available opponents to a limited area. Much ingenuity was required to get football teams transported by bus, train or shared cars using precious petrol coupons. There was one away school we played that required the team to walk two miles to the opponent's playing fields. Probably a good thing as we would arrive limbered up despite the whining and claims of pre-game exhaustion.

Since we lived in the country, our activities outside of school hours offered more opportunity for a variety of pastimes than for boys living in the cities. Much of what I found to do was associated with the farm. Despite this, I can recall many an occasion when I would complain "I am bored, I've got nothing to do." That was rubbish of course as there was an unending opportunity for enjoyable activities. What I was really saying was that I needed a companion with whom I could while away the hours. My brothers were a lot older than me. Mick, the next one up from me, was five years my senior and had little taste for hanging out with me.

My pal Richard was sometimes available to spend time with me but, as he grew older, his passion for farming was a stronger magnet. At the drop of a hat, he was available for any activity on the farm. Being that bit older than me, it was understandable that he would make that choice. I am glad that he was so devoted to agriculture because he made a great success of his chosen career in later life. At the time, I was somewhat piqued that so often I was his second choice.

My mother would step in to help solve my supposed loneliness and would often arrange for a friend to bicycle over to spend the day with me or for me to go to someone else's house for the day. The truth is I really had a pretty good life and like most boys of that age, was not appreciative enough of the opportunities I truly had.

There were times when I could be useful on the farm when labour intensive jobs had to be done. Cattle and sheep had to be moved from one pasture to another when they had grazed out the available feed. This involved herding the animals down the country lanes and even on the main village street. Since the farm was spread out with some fields two miles away from others, the sheep and cattle drives were hazardous both with the traffic and from the devastation the livestock could cause if they escaped off the roads and into villagers' gardens.

The strategy for moving them on the public roads was to have one person in front to keep them from running on ahead. There was usually a need for two more workers to cover each side of the road to shut garden gates or at least to prevent side escapes by the nervous animals. One more person would bring up the rear. That amounted to an ideal crew of six people but often we were short two or three helpers.

On a few occasions things went horribly wrong. The problem would be that one or two cattle or sheep would break away through a gap on the side of the road. Once one animal established an escape route the rest would stampede in the same direction. The devastation that a herd of twenty cattle or even sheep could cause in a resident's flower or vegetable garden was enough to make the homeowner weep. After much shouting and beating with sticks, we would eventually get the herd back on the road but after their taste of freedom it was like trying to contain the bulls in Pamplona during the annual Running of the Bulls Festival.

After an incident like this, the negotiation for repair of the damage was always difficult. Happily, most villagers were country folk who understood the needs of the farmer; however, real costs were involved not just from a monetary point of view but in terms of the homeowner's precious garden vegetables. Everyone was encouraged to 'Dig for *Victory*' to supplement their food rations. My father was able to help out with vegetables from our own substantial vegetable garden or from the farm crops. A couple of chickens and a brace or two of rabbits with a few veggies could go a long way to quieting the righteous indignation of the homeowners.

My role in these cattle and sheep drives was usually to drive the car from the point of departure to the destination so that the drovers could be picked up when the job was done. As a ten-year-old, I could barely see over the steering wheel and my feet had trouble reaching the pedals. The progress of the drive was usually slow so I was able to keep the car in first gear. Changing with the stick shift was not usually required. The village policeman would look the other way as I drove past. It was not until I finally passed my driving test at the age of sixteen that he deliberately pulled me over demanding to see my licence. There was a twinkle in his eye as he did so. He knew very well that I had obtained it only a few days earlier. He kept a pretty good tab on all the goings-on in the village and used good judgement in his application of the law.

The first two weeks of July were cherry picking season. There was an orchard of about four acres directly behind the farm house. They were big old trees producing the sweet orange and white Bing cherries, the dark red sweet variety called, I believe "Imperial". We also had the sour Montmorency cooking cherries. The cherry crop was always a gamble. If it rained when the cherries were ripe and still on the trees, the fruit would split and had little market value as they would not keep well and looked as though a bird had pecked them. If you didn't pick the cherries fast enough when they were ripe, the birds would beat you to it. So, when the two-week season was upon us every available man, woman and child was accepted as a cherry picker.

Pickers could eat all they wanted on the first morning of picking because it was guaranteed that they would not want to put another cherry in their mouths after the first hour of pigging out. The trees were old and high and it needed long 40 foot ladders to reach the top branches. If you couldn't stand heights, you wouldn't volunteer for picking cherries.

One of the jobs I was given was to try and keep the starlings and other birds away from the orchard. To frighten them off, we would hang ropes of what we called 'bangers' from some of the trees. Bangers consisted of a slow burning rope with loud explosive charges every three inches. As the rope smoldered upwards, it would set off the gunpowder charges every fifteen minutes or so. I was also allowed to roam the orchard with a small bore .410 shot gun when the pickers were not there. When I shot a starling robbing the cherries, I would hang the dead bird by a string from the tree as a warning to other birds.

Another occasion when all hands were required on deck at the farm was at sheep -shearing and dipping time. Shearing the wool with a motorized set of clippers was hard work as it had to be done one-on-one between the shearer and each sheep. It was a job only for the strongest of men. A struggling 130 lb. sheep was hard to handle. A team of professionals would travel from farm to farm to do this but during the war such professionals were not always available and my brothers would have to help out. It was easy to spot which sheep my brothers clipped as the poor creatures looked scruffy in their summer-style coats and had little cuts showing red in various places.

All adult sheep were treated at least once a year for the control of lice, ticks, blow fly and other pests. A convenient time to do this was after the sheep had been sheared. The process involved submerging each sheep into a bath of chemicals in a concrete dipping trough. A team was required to catch the sheep and drop them into the bath of blue coloured chemical soup. They were dipped under water with a long-handled double hook as they swam towards the exit ramp. There they joined the rest of the flock spluttering and shaking the solution off their backs. All of this was accomplished with a cacophony of bleating matched only by the noise on the day the lambs were separated from their mothers.

I was never quite sure why but at sheep dipping time a policeman had to be in attendance. I think it must have been because of the toxicity of the chemicals used in the sheep dip and the possibility that the dangerous fluids were not handled with sufficient care.

The harvest field made demands on all of us. With wheat, oats and barley fields all ripening in the same few weeks in July and August, it was always a hectic time. The weather complicated matters even more as the cut grain should not be tied into sheaves if it was damp as the grain spoiled if the air did not get to it and dry it out.

My role as a ten-year-old was usually to sit on the seat of the Massey or McCormick reaper/binder harvesting machines which circled the field around the ever-diminishing standing corn. My job was to see that the cut grain crop travelled smoothly on the rotating canvas platform into the mechanical tying equipment under my seat. The crop would then be ejected out the other side as a tied sheaf. It was not a very demanding job under perfect conditions but when the standing wheat had been knocked down by the rain and wind it was a struggle to get the crop going through the machine without jamming up. To prevent this, I had a six-foot stick to straighten out any out-of-line bundles. Frequently, I had to wallop the metal part of the binder to get the tractor driver to stop so that we could sort out the mess. Broken binder twine for tying the sheaves was another frequent stoppage requiring it to be re-threaded through the various moving parts. In the 1940's, we were still using mechanical equipment that was first developed in the 19th century but somehow we muddled through the process of providing grain for the bread of the nation.

A time-honoured custom in the countryside was the practice of gleaning. It was particularly beneficial in WWII. Many of the local residents raised chickens in their back yards to supplement their food supply. After a field had been harvested and the sheaves of wheat removed to the stack yard, the women and children from the village would spread out over the fields gathering up any leftover grain lying on the ground. This was valuable feed for the chickens at home. If it wasn't picked up, it would simply germinate in the soil or be eaten by wildlife.

Threshing time usually took place in the winter months. When the sheaves of grain were taken off the harvest fields they were transported to a stack or rick yard to await the threshing season when the grain was separated from the stalks. Before starting to build a grain stack, bundles of small branches or '*faggots*' would be laid on the ground to keep the bottom sheaves off the damp ground. On this base, the sheaves were carefully placed in circular lines for a round stack or in straight rows for a square or straight-sided stack. There was an art to this building process and the chief stacker was careful to do a neat job as inferior work was there for all to see if his efforts started to lean or even collapse. His lack of skill would be there for the weeks and months to come much to the teasing of his mates over a pint in the pub.

The threshing of the wheat, oats or barley from the storage stacks took place in early winter. This was long before the invention of the combine harvester. Combines complete the threshing process while the grain is still standing in the fields. In the 1940's, we still had to go through the laborious process of cutting, storing and threshing in three separate stages. The threshing team had to be booked ahead of time as the big steam engine towing the threshing machine trundled around from farm to farm.

When all the equipment had been set up, the stack was taken apart one sheaf at a time and then fed into the threshing machine. It was hard and dusty work. As I grew older, I would sometimes take a position as one of the threshing team but it was far more fun as a boy when I could take Pepper, our fox terrier, and go mousing on the stack as it was dismantled. I would be armed with a stick and Pepper would be keenly waiting to do a quick execution job. As the farm worker used his pitch fork to lift the sheaf, we would be at the ready. Often there would be one or two mice exposed and Pepper would pounce and chomp and I would whack them with my stick. There were usually hundreds of mice in every stack. The longer the stack had been there the more mice took up residence. So long as we did not get in the way of the worker lifting the sheaves, we were welcome to rain carnage on the mouse and rat population.

It used to bother me that so many mice had been living among the grains of wheat that we were soon going to eat as bread. I believe the grain was cleaned in some way after it left the farm and was shipped to the corn merchant. I trust that some attempt was made to clean out the mouse droppings and other undesirable bits and pieces before the grain was ground into flour. Still, I do know that buyers of the sacks of wheat would pick up handfuls of the grain and run it through their fingers as they inspected the grain for plumpness and quality and sniffed it to check for mould and perhaps that distinct smell of mouse contamination.

Cattle driving, sheep shearing and dipping, harvest time, cherry picking and threshing times were the occasions when my help was required on the farm. But there was plenty of time between these demanding occasions for more innocent recreation.

Ash Poles and Eels

They are slippery little buggers. Eels that is. But they provided me with a particularly warm and intimate opportunity to get to know my father. Dad was a shy man although he was known to enjoy a boozy lunch with his farming friends on market days in Rochester. He and his pals would do whatever business they had to take care of on Tuesday mornings and then retire to the Bull Inn on The High Street in Rochester. This was Charles Dickens country and the Bull was an old coaching inn complete with an arched entrance leading into the courtyard where the horses were changed in earlier days. In the shadow of Rochester Cathedral, it was a setting right out of one of those Victorian paintings.

Since I was the youngest of seven children, it was not surprising that I was not able to spend too many hours in my father's company. He had experienced more major events and difficult times than most other men. Dad went through WWI in the trenches in France while serving with the Royal West Kent Regiment. That must have been a terrible experience for him and I believe it influenced his personality. Understandably so: he was awarded the Military Cross for bravery when leading his platoon into enemy lines. They captured twelve German soldiers. He was wounded in this action but recovered without any serious after effects.

After his WWI experiences, the Great Depression, and the stress of yet another war, it was not surprising that it left its mark.

Millions of other men had to endure the same series of traumatic ordeals and often the effect on their personalities was more pronounced so I consider that Dad came through it rather well. A little shyness was quite understandable and in some ways was quite endearing. He was a very decent and honest person who raised a large family under trying conditions. He carried the air of authority well and his wishes were others' commands both at home and at work. With a workforce on the farm of about a half dozen men plus a family of seven, he was required to shoulder substantial responsibilities.

One day in April 1943, I had him to myself. It was his idea. He planned an outing just for the two of us.

"Let's take the day off and go fishing" he said, much to my surprise.

It was to be fishing of a different sort. The evening before the appointed day we did two things. First, we took a billhook and walked down the nearby hedgerow and cut two poles from ash trees, each about 12 feet long. My father insisted that they should be ash saplings or shoots as ash is a strong yet flexible wood ideal for a make-shift fishing pole. It was a wood used on the farm for making sheep hurdles and fencing and was harvested for this purpose just like any other crop on the farm.

Then we took a spade and found a moist spot in the garden where we dug the soil over looking for big fat earthworms. We left the poles and the worms in the barn ready for our fishing expedition the next day.

Before setting out in the car in the morning, Dad persuaded my mother to lend him the largest sewing needle she could find in her sewing basket. Rummaging about in that same basket he found a reel of strong, thick, cotton thread. Next, we cut two lengths of binder twine each about 10 feet long. This is a strong twine used on the farm for tying sheaves of wheat, barley or oats in the harvest field and for all manner of fix and repair jobs. We tied the lengths of binder twine to the ends of the ash poles. Putting all our equipment in the car we set off for a place called Reculver on the north Kent coast about 30 minutes away.

During the war, very few beaches were open to the public as all possible landing places for a German invasion were protected with explosive mines hidden in the sand or shingle, however, there were a few seashores which were unsuitable for an invasion force to land and, therefore, left free of mines. The shoreline near Reculver was steep and thus unsuitable for enemy forces trying to establish a beachhead. In addition, there was an old Martello tower a mile away overlooking the coastline. It was an ideal defensive stronghold and was probably equipped with all kinds of guns and anti-invasion weapons. Martello towers were built around much of Britain's coastline in the early 19th century at the time of the Napoleonic wars. The shoreline there was not flying the red flag, symbol of a mined area, ergo it was not an out-of-bounds area. It was one of the few beachfronts where we could go fishing. It was also a very remote area which meant that we would not be troubled by coast guard volunteers enquiring what we were up to, not that we were doing anything wrong.

Upon arrival at the shore, we took the needle and thread and pierced the worms so that the thread ran through the body of the worms from end to end. Not a pleasant job and no fun for the worms. When we had about a dozen worms on each length of thread, we gathered the long strings of them into two bundles about the size of a small tennis ball and tied each bundle onto the ends of the binder twine on each pole. This was our combination of bait and concealed hook. Advancing down the wet shingle of the beach, we dropped the bundle of worms into the sea alongside the wooden breakwaters. It was just a moment before the tip of my pole was dragged down.

"Quick, flick the pole up and over your head" said my Dad.

I did so but nothing came up on the end of the line except the bundle of worms. My strike was not executed at the critical moment and I came up empty handed.

Just then my Dad's pole jerked downwards. With a rapid flick of his wrist the pole flew up and the line snaked over his head. There was a flash of silver as something was attached to the bait bundle. It was an eel. As it landed, it opened its mouth and let go of the worm ball. Its teeth had been caught in the thread inside the worms when the eel bit the tasty bundle. No hook was involved, just the snagging of the eel's teeth on the cotton thread. The skill required was to judge just the right moment to jerk the pole up and over your head with the eel's teeth entangled in the thread.

We may have got the eel out of the water on to land but that was only the beginning of the fun. The shingle beach was still wet from the waves that had broken over it. It was a steep slope from where the eel landed down to the water's edge. Eels are covered in a slime making it very hard to pick them up so they slipped easily through our fingers.

The chase was now on. The eel was determined to make its way back to the safety of the water. With quick motions of its snake-like body, it started to wriggle its way back down the sloping wet shingle at a surprisingly fast speed. Equally determined were my Dad and I as we tried to catch it. We grabbed it several times but always it managed to slide out from our grasp, thanks to the slipperiness of its body. This eel made its way safely back to the salt water.

An observer would have been intrigued at the spectacle we presented. A 50-year old man and a ten year-old boy were slipping and sliding their way down the slick shingle slope. Occasional lunges into the shingle were accompanied by shrieks of laughter. The episode ended with both participants sitting on their backsides in the surf doubled up with laughter.

Round one went to the eels. Round two was a different story. I learned the knack of recognizing the right moment to strike when the eel bit onto the bait. With just the right timing, I quickly flicked the eels over my head as my father had demonstrated. With the help of an old grain sack we found in the back of the car, we improved our grip on the slippery eels. Our catch record improved as we were able to hang on to about half the eels we managed to throw back up the beach. Soon we had a bucket full of writhing eels still very much alive despite being out of the water. As part of their life cycle, eels can travel over land when they need to find a new habitat in which to live. Unlike fish, they can survive a long time being out of water.

Soon we had a catch of twenty or more large eels measuring 18 to 24 inches long. On average, they must have weighed more than a pound each as we didn't waste our energy on the small ones, besides which the little eels were even harder to grip. We kept the writhing, squirming victims in a large bucket. We had more than we had expected to catch. The problem was to know what to do with them. They are a very nutritious food but preparing them for our own supper was more than we cared to undertake. Jellied eels were a favourite dish, especially in the east end of London. Smoked eels were considered a delicacy, too. But we had just had three hours of fun catching them and were soaked with sea water and covered in eel slime. The prospect of taking them home and spending another hour or two cutting their heads off and skinning them definitely did not appeal. Apart from that, we were not sure how well they would be received at home. Not everyone has a taste for eels, especially if the family had been exposed to the messy process of beheading and skinning live eels in the kitchen before cooking them.

As we loaded the car, my father came up with a good idea. In the nearby town of Gravesend there was one narrow street that led down to the River Thames. I believe it was called the High Street. In those days, it ran down to the water so it was close to where the shrimp boats and other fishing vessels unloaded their catches. At that time, there were a number of fish shops lining the street. Today, I doubt if you will find even one there as that messy, bustling street has become gentrified and the fish can now be found only in the supermarkets.

Dad's idea was to go straight there and see if we could trade our heavy load of eels for some more desirable sea food. Arriving at the High Street, we parked the car and wandered down the hill looking for a fish shop that looked as though they would take our catch. We hadn't gone far before we spotted one that seemed a likely candidate. On the marble display slab the fishmonger had displayed cockles and mussels and even the little shellfish called winkles that you eat with a pin by unwinding the body of the creature from within its spiral shell. This is the mollusc that has given rise to the term "to winkle something out". They had all kinds of fish including my mother's favourite, smoked haddock. They even had cooked jellied eels in pint jars and sections of smoked eels for sale. This looked like a likely spot to take our catch of still-wriggling eels.

The car wouldn't fit down the narrow street with all the people and carts blocking it so we carried the still wriggling eels in the bucket down to the fishmonger. Somewhat to our surprise and pleasure, he showed an interest in what we had to offer. The eels were obviously very fresh and were the ideal size for eating. But Dad had plans other than just trying to sell them.

"What if I suggested to you that we would like to give you these in exchange for enough smoked haddock for supper for my family of six", he said.

My mother was not the only one who loved smoked haddock as we all enjoyed it too. She served it gently cooked in milk and butter with one of our free-range eggs poached on top. Delicious.

The fishmonger thought for a moment, picked up the bucket to assess the weight of its contents and replied, "OK I will give you the haddock in a straight exchange".

"Sounds good", said my Dad, "but I would love to have some shrimp. Could you possibly include a pint of cooked shrimp as well?"

These were the small local shrimp that were sold by the pint rather than by the pound. They were inexpensive and a favourite

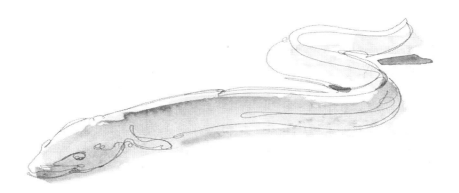

with the locals for tea. We would peel them and have them on toast. It was a labour of love but their fresh salty flavour made the long process of peeling them worth the effort.

"OK," said the fishmonger.

"You've got a deal," said my father.

So, we swapped about thirty pounds of eels for about three pounds of smoked haddock and a pint of shrimps. Not a bad deal considering we really didn't know what to do with the live eels. We had the fun of catching them and now would be welcomed back home with some good-eating fish rather than the evil-looking eels.

"Look what we caught", we said on arrival back home. For some reason, my mother didn't quite buy our story. Eventually she winkled the true story out of us.

"Pity," said my Mum with a twinkle in her eye, "I really would have loved fried eels for supper."

Eel Pie and Mash was the working man's favourite meal in the 18th and 19th centuries as it was cheap and full of nutrition. At that time, eels could be caught in the Thames in the heart of London. Pollution has since made life in the river impossible for this hardy creature. Fish and Chips has replaced this once popular dish but with the fish being caught in cleaner waters elsewhere. However, there are still a few restaurants in London bearing the name *Eel Pie Shop* in the east end of London where the true cockneys live and keep the tradition going.

That was a not-so-classic fishing story but the real story was that I had seen another side of my father's personality for the first time. Yes, he was a shy man but underneath that reserve there was someone who could not only enjoy a day's outing to go fishing but was able to let himself go and have some light-hearted fun. It was good to know that on the other side of that authority figure there was a lighter and more lovable person too. For that ten-year-old, it was an eye-opener to share those precious moments of scrambling, slipping, sliding, and laughing our way down a wet shingle beach in pursuit of some slippery, slimy eels. We were both ten years old that day.

It was a brief moment to be treasured and remembered these seventy-five years on.

Unlocking the Love Story

A century after the event, it is difficult to muster all the facts, but it seems that a classic romance story unfolded as the First World War ended in 1918. My parents were married in 1917. The events leading to the ceremony, while lacking some details, have all the traces of a classic love story.

My father was invalided out of the army in 1917. His wounds to his leg were healed and he was able to lead a normal civilian life. At first, he thought about becoming a chemist or a pharmacist. I can attest to this as the garden shed at home had rows of glass jars on the shelves containing relatively harmless chemicals. My interest was in the sulphur and saltpeter (potassium nitrate). With a little charcoal shaved from burned wood, I spent many hours creating my version of gunpowder or black powder as it was known in the days of muzzle loaders and cannon balls.

The goldfish in the garden pond suffered many traumatic days when I recreated the sinking of the German pocket battleships, the Bismarck and the Tirpitz. Sometimes I had plastic replicas of warships but more often my fleets consisted of scraps of wood nailed together and imbued with a lot of imagination. A little of my gunpowder sprinkled on the upper deck and ignited by a match would sometimes simulate naval warfare. A brief fizzle, a spark or two and a puff of smoke was all I needed to reproduce battle on the high seas. This was much to the surprise of the orange coy fish that chose to investigate this intrusion into their tranquil life.

My father's early experimentation with a career in chemistry failed to produce results. Instead, he took over the family farm.

It is at this point that my mother entered the scene. Doris McClure was one of three daughters of Dr. Thomas McClure, a physician in Luton, Bedfordshire. Perhaps because it was nearby, Doris enrolled in the Reading Dairy School which today is known as the School of Food Chain Sciences at the University of Reading. Her sister, Eileen, was also studying at the Dairy School. Eileen later emigrated to Canada where she continued her studies at the Ontario Agricultural College.

It is not clear when or where Doris first met my father, but we can presume it was during a visit to Kent in 1916. There is a gap in recorded history at this time, but it is likely the first spark of romance was kindled on this visit.

There followed a period for Doris that is hard to explain. At about this time, even though the war raged on, she boarded a steamer and sailed to stay with her uncle in Uganda. Her uncle was an engineer charged with building the railway from Kenya to Uganda. This project became famous for the large number of indigenous workers on the line who were killed by lions. The book, The *Man-eaters of Tsavo*, written by John Henry Patterson, was about the loss of life during the construction. It was later made into a movie of the same name.

We know little of why Doris, just twenty years old, went on this trip. It may have been to help her uncle's family by escorting one of his children back to join the family in Uganda after attending boarding school in England. It could have been just for the adventure. Could it have been to get over a failed love affair; possibly an initial dalliance with my father? We will never know! What we do know is that while in Uganda she met an officer in the East African Rifles. This was a British battalion recruited from the white settlers in Kenya and Uganda. It was not long before their engagement was announced. It was not to last as rumours began circulating that the officer had had a liaison with a local resident and offspring had resulted.

It didn't take long for the bush telegraph to transmit the news of the breakup to England. My father leapt into action. Within hours, a telegram sped on its way to Uganda. "Come home and marry me" were the cryptic words that were pasted onto the simple sheet in the little buff envelope.

The steamer trunk was repacked and the next steamship out of Mombasa bore the bride-to-be back home. Within a few months the marriage banns were read and before the end of 1917 the happy couple took up residence back on the farm where they lived for the next 46 years.

Now, isn't that a true romance!

The Role of "Auntie"

"Lights out" was the daily call at 9:00 pm. while I was at boarding school. The corridor lights were doused and, one by one, book markers were inserted to keep the place in novels or corners of pages turned down. Bedside lamps in the sleeping cubicles were reluctantly turned off. For one or two of us, this was a call to reach under the mattress and extract one ear piece of a headset, a ten-foot length of aerial wire and a tiny device known as a crystal radio.

One end of the aerial wire was suspended out the window and the other end attached to the crystal. Lying on my stomach with the little radio set just peeping out from my pillow, I was able to tune in to the BBC while ready at any moment to slide the contraption back under the pillow if footsteps of a prefect were heard coming down the corridor.

There was a knack to tuning in the crystal radio. It needed a delicate touch to twiddle the probe against the crystal so that the right frequency was found. If you got it right, the radio program would be received quite clearly but at a low volume through the one ear piece speaker.

There was a thriving underground industry within the school for the assembly of this very simple device. I imagine the resourceful student who put the sets together went on to be a successful entrepreneur in later life. On the other hand, he may have ended up incarcerated for other clandestine industries. His business life cycle at school was inevitably discovered, shut down, and the instigator subjected to school detentions. My crystal set was confiscated and I did not see it again until I was on the way home at the end of that school term.

This little exercise in communication illustrates the importance of the radio in the war. We all hungered for news and entertainment every day. At least until 1943, when the Americans arrived on British shores, the word 'radio' was another term for the BBC.

The BBC, the British Broadcasting Corporation, was known affectionately as 'Auntie'. This was a term that aptly described the sort of maiden aunt role that the BBC earned through its prudish, scolding manner with which it addressed the British people. It was the mouth piece for the government and controlled the content of most of the entertainment provided to the population throughout the war.

Ultra-conservative in its policies, it had trouble keeping up with the tastes of the people in a rapidly changing environment. Despite this, it was listened to avidly and was relied upon for accurate news on the state of the war. It was the only communication medium that could reach all the people. The Greek dramatist Aeschylus wrote in 450 BC, "in war, truth is the first casualty." No doubt there was some manipulation of the facts but the BBC was considered to be more reliable in its reporting than any other news source.

It was the radio that kept the nation informed. Yes, there were the daily newspapers, both morning and evening editions, but with the shortage of newsprint their daily broadsheets had space for little more than the scores of planes shot down, army advances or retreats, and highly censored news of naval engagements. What space was left on their pages was largely taken up with government announcements and propaganda.

Radio broadcasting was limited to the services of the BBC on two major networks, the Home Service and the Forces Network. The Home Service was very 'old school' conservative and, consequently, very dull but looked to for solid news reports. Just about every home in Britain gathered around the home hearth every evening for the all-important nine o'clock evening news. The rest of their programming was very formal, limiting the content to talks and classical and dance music. Initially, jazz music was banned as it was thought to be too American and degrading.

The BBC Forces Programme soon out-rated the Home Service as the troops and factory workers much preferred the lighter programming of this network. The taste for this lighter style had been initiated by some of the foreign based radio stations with programmes in English beamed to the UK.

The most listened-to of these stations was Radio Luxembourg which had picked up the programming style of many of the American commercial stations. Jazz and other popular dance music coupled with a lighter and friendlier tone of the announcers contrasted favourably with the heavier tones of the BBC. It was the demise of Radio Luxembourg in 1940 that finally created the opportunity for the BBC to introduce this more popular programming. The BBC picked up the style of Radio Luxembourg in the Forces network and eventually changed the name to the Light Programme.

Radio Luxembourg had been slowly capturing the British audiences in the 1930's but in 1940 the station went off air with the advance of the Nazi forces. The tables were turned when the Germans took over as they started broadcasting German propaganda in English toward the UK. The most famous of their broadcasters was William Joyce, better known as 'Lord Haw-Haw'. He was American born but lived in Ireland and England where he was a member of the Fascist Party. In 1939, he fled to Germany. His weekly broadcasts were designed to undermine the confidence of the British troops and people. After the war, he was tried for treason and was hanged on January 3, 1946.

Lord Haw-Haw played a role similar to 'Tokyo Rose', who broadcast from Japan to the American and Allied troops in the Pacific. Both broadcasters attempted to undermine the confidence of the Allied troops. Iva Toguri d'Aquino, the principle broadcaster playing the part of Tokyo Rose, chose to do this by telling the American GI's that their wives and sweethearts were seeing other men back in the US. She was born in America but was stranded in Japan after Pearl Harbour. The Japanese interned her and persuaded her to undertake the broadcasts. At war's end, she was brought back to the US and tried for treason. She served six years in jail but was eventually pardoned by President Ford in 1976.

The arrival of American troops added to the change in attitude at the BBC. It wasn't long before the Americans established their own radio broadcasting on AFN, the American Forces Network. The first broadcast was on July 3rd, 1943, with equipment borrowed from the BBC. In typical fashion, the BBC was only partially co-operative and required AFN to carry some of the BBC programming. However, by D-Day in 1944, AFN was fully independent and listened to by much of the British public as well as the American troops for whom the broadcasts were really intended.

The competition between the networks created a wealth of artistic talent and a wide range in styles. By the war's end, audiences were familiar with the popular singers and entertainers from both sides of the Atlantic. The talents of the artists played an enormous part in keeping up the spirits and morale of the British people throughout WWII. The same can be said for all English-speaking people around the world who relied upon the shortwave broadcasts of the BBC for news and support.

On the German side, the troops eagerly tuned in to their own radio broadcasts. There is the interesting case of one popular love song, called Lili Marlene, whose haunting music and nostalgic lyrics were favourites with both the German and the British troops. The melody and the words were first composed in German in 1938 and then translated into English in 1940. By a strange coincidence, the singer most noted for singing the English version was Marlene Dietrich who was born in Germany but became an American citizen and Hollywood star.

Spies were embedded on both sides in the war and the BBC played an important part in communicating with our spies through coded messages to them within the daily broadcasts. Members of the Resistance in France and other occupied countries also relied on information transmitted through regular broadcasting from the BBC. Listeners were sometimes surprised to hear out of context statements on air that made little sense except to those in occupied Europe who were waiting to receive their coded instructions.

The radio services of the BBC, while derided by many, played a unique role in maintaining the morale of the British forces and people at home and abroad throughout the war years. The BBC may have been dubbed "Auntie" for its prudish policies but it was also a favourite family member of the Brits.

Hop Holidays

The Hop Holiday was an annual event during which thousands of east-enders from London left their crowded one-up-one-down houses in the docklands of London and headed for a paying holiday in the Kent countryside. In the months of August and September, this mass exodus enabled whole families to take a fresh air holiday harvesting in the hop gardens.

There were two hop kilns on our family farm. They were typical iconic Kentish oast houses or hop kilns as we called them. They were round, two story buildings built out of flint stones. Flints were cemented together in a similar manner to bricks but with a black and white distinctive appearance unique to the county of Kent. These stones occur naturally in the chalk soils of the county. Each hop kiln had a venting cone at the pinnacle of the roof to release the moist air from the hops drying on the second floor below. Even in 1939 both of the buildings were in poor condition and it had been a long time since they had been used for their original purpose of drying hops. The term 'oast house' is derived from the Dutch language where it means 'drying house' and that quite simply was all they were good for.

The hop kilns were an indication that at some time in the past, hops had been grown on the farm. In 1939, they were used occasionally as a stable, for giving shelter to sheep or cattle or as a temporary storage place for farm machinery. The floors were earthen and usually covered with a layer of straw. We seldom entered them except to check if the chickens had chosen to lay their eggs there. On more than one occasion, a broody hen had marched her family of newborn baby chicks out of her hideaway there for all to admire.

Hops were grown on other farms in the area with the nearest hop garden about three miles away in the Dickensian village of Cobham. The harvest time for hops is during late August and early September. The harvest of the grain crops was usually over for us by the middle of August. The wheat, barley and oat crops were stored in stacks in the fields where they had been grown. The grain was still on the stalks at this stage awaiting the threshing machine which would do the rounds of the neighbourhood farms later in the year. Consequently, there was a relatively quiet time on the farm during this period and before back-to-school time.

Since it was always tempting to add a little to the family income, we arranged to participate in the hop harvest in 1943. Apart from earning a little extra money, helping out with the hop picking was reputed to be a lot of fun despite the hard work involved. Since we were a family of seven children, some of whom had time on their hands, it was an interesting way to experience something new and involve the younger members of the family as all ages could participate.

Considering we had a farm of our own to run you would think that we had enough to do at home. Farm help was hard to obtain during the war years and I believe my father knew the owner of the hop garden and learned he needed extra help. After the grain harvest in August, it was a quieter time for a farm such as ours so my mother gathered up as many of us as she could find and set out for some fun and a little pocket money.

Little did we realize what a big commitment it was to be assigned a hop bin in the hop field. On the other hand, it was a unique experience for us country dwellers to work cheek by jowl with large Cockney families from London. They were a rough lot but fun-loving and friendly.

The hop bines grow up long strings attached to overhead wires. When the hop flowers or cones are ready for picking, the supervisor, balancing on ten-foot stilts, cuts down the long strands of string to which the hop bines have attached themselves. Two or three of these bines are laid over the big hessian bag or poke that is hung between a wooden framework at ground level. The pokes are like giant pillowcases about three feet across and six feet long. The hop picker's family gathers on each side of the bag and starts to pick off the hop cones by hand, dropping them into the poke.

The hop cones are very light and it took us a long time to fill the big sack. Since the pickers were paid a set amount for each filled sack, the occasional kick upwards with a good boot into the underside of the giant pillow helped to fluff up the hops. The trick was to increase the volume rather than the weight of the harvested hops.

Whereas we went back home every night, the majority of the London families camped out in makeshift tents or crude wooden sheds known as hop houses provided by the farmer. The hours were long but it was a strict rule that all work would cease at 5:00 pm. This was the excuse to start the evening entertainment. Families gathered round their cooking fires and socialized while the evening meal was prepared. Food was very basic although poaching wild game was a frequent method of augmenting the family dinners. The men folk would quietly set up snares for the local rabbits. The local foxes were often blamed for the disappearance of an unusually large number of chickens from the pens of nearby residents in hop picking season, however the trail of feathers would more likely lead to the hop garden than into any fox's den.

Young and old would get together and a communal singsong would develop perhaps led by a mouth organ player. As the evening grew darker, the older folk would drift off to the nearest pub. The local publican welcomed the extra cash in the till but. at hop picking time, his best tankards were put away and jam jars substituted, as many of the best glasses found their way out of the pubs and into the hop huts.

Working in the hop gardens was one of the safer places to be in an air raid as the avenues of tall hop bines acted as good camouflage against any bloody-minded fighter pilot anxious to use us as a target. The bines were no protection against falling shrapnel from the overhead flak. We would huddle under the pokes filled with the hop cones if the action became too hot. In fact, this would give little protection against falling bits of metal so the protection was more from a psychological point of view than in reality.

There is a distinctive smell to life in the hop gardens. Hops are used in the brewing of beer to counteract the sweetness of the fermented grain. The bitterness of the hops not only balances the flavour of the brew but also adds a distinct aroma. With row upon row of the bines all around us that same smell was strong and not unpleasant. It also had the effect of clearing the nostrils and perhaps even the head after a night at the pub. Of secondary importance perhaps was its ability to mask the ever-present body odour of the great unwashed of our Cockney friends. All that fresh air was not accompanied by the equivalent in bathing facilities.

At ten years old in 1943, I was not aware of the ' goings on' in the social life of the hop pickers. Later study of the surprisingly large media coverage of life in the hop gardens revealed that the four weeks of freedom from the cramped living conditions and prying eyes of the dockland neighbours liberated the hop pickers in more ways than one. Apparently, some of the ladies, with their husbands left behind in the city or away on war service, felt the need to try some new experiences. There was a clandestine custom of taking on a 'hop husband' probably from among the local male farm workers. Such affairs were referred to as a couple having 'hopped over the bine'. Evidence of such a custom would be revealed nine months later when the parentage of the offspring would have been in some doubt but accepted as one of the outcomes of wartime influences.

Sometimes, German prisoners of war were delivered in army trucks to help with the hop harvest. For them, it was a welcome break from the boredom of the prison camps. Socializing with the families that they and their brothers-in-arms had been bombing did put a crimp in their acceptance by the Londoners. Most of the POWs in 1943 were airmen who had been shot down over Kent and the southeast of England. Kent was in the direct path of the Luftwaffe raids and the frequent wailing of the air raid sirens was a constant reminder that the POWs, until recently, had been bombing the hop pickers' homes.

Over time, the POW's were accepted as just people like their neighbours filling the hop bins on each side. The chilly ice was eventually broken. Since the prisoners had to return to their camp each evening, they didn't have the opportunity to join in the socializing in the evenings. Nonetheless, with the shortage of men among the hop pickers, liaisons were often established. The youth and fitness of the POWs added a little spice to their natural attraction for the ladies.

As the final bines were stripped of their green fruits, many of the hop farms held a Hop Festival with lots of food, beer and cider and traditional ceremonies. At these events, a Hop Queen would be crowned. In September, the pickers were relieved to take a break from the long hours in the fields and return to their customary way of life in the city. They appreciated the extra money they took home, though the rate of pay was low. This was extra money they could use to buy needed clothing for the family before the onset of winter.

Family friendships were coming to an end for another year and promises were made to pick alongside new and old friends again next year. The hop farmers were always glad of the labour and addresses were taken so that hop cards could be mailed out by the farmers to ensure a steady supply of help the following year.

It was hard work but the same pickers usually returned each season to enjoy the only fresh air holiday many were able to afford.

Collecting Things

What goes up must come down. It wasn't just what the Germans brought over to drop on us but what our side sent up that accounted for much of the fallout from the sky.

Admittedly, the German bombs were more explosive but the fallout from the sky that the British fired to bring down the enemy was almost as dangerous. Exploding anti-aircraft shells broke up into pieces ranging in size from less than one inch to three inches. These pieces were jagged bits of metal falling from a height of perhaps 10,000 feet and were therefore, a potentially lethal weapon. Some parts of the shell were larger. The nose cone of an anti-aircraft shell usually stayed in one piece measuring perhaps two inches high with a base of about the same size. With its pointed tip, it could penetrate to a fatal degree.

The farm buildings and our house were roofed with slate tiles. During a raid, any falling pieces of shrapnel measuring an inch or more could shatter those slate tiles. You can imagine how nasty that would be if it was your head on which one of those pieces landed. During a raid, we would stand just inside the back door overlooking the farm buildings and listen for the whistle of falling bits and pieces. If there was a light 'ping' on a roof, we would know that the roof was still intact. A louder 'clang' followed by the sound of broken slates sliding down the roof told us we would have to get out the ladder and replace a tile or two.

Maybe it was because of the danger that shrapnel posed which caused small boys and even girls to want to collect it. We should have turned it in to be melted down and re-used but the appeal of a shrapnel collection and its trading value with our friends proved to be too strong a temptation.

Scrap metal and any metal railings or fences that were not required for safety reasons were requisitioned by the government for turning into weapons. At the front of our farmhouse, there were some iron railings at the point where our property bordered on the road. They had been there as long as anyone could remember. The railings were hidden inside an evergreen hedge that had overgrown it. There must have been some officials driving around the countryside looking for such sources of metal because one day a note appeared at our door saying that the fence was required for the war effort. A few days later a crew with an acetylene torch arrived and cut it down. Happily, they were able to do this without destroying the hedge so we didn't miss the metal railings.

Small boys are driven to collecting things. You only have to empty out the pockets of their short pants to disclose an odd assortment of seemingly useless things to an adult but which are treasures to the boys. The selection of items can include anything. Maybe a marble or two, a sticky sweet long past its best-before date, a key that just might open a pirate's treasure chest when one is eventually found, a fake cigarette with the end painted red to simulate it being alight, or even a bent cigarette card featuring a photo of Lana Turner. On a sexier level, you might have found a torn-out section of the Daily Mirror showing the cartoon strip 'Just Jane' in yet another situation in which her clothes seem to have fallen off. Pretty mild stuff really but titillating to boys of that age.

Comics were usually published weekly, were printed on poor quality news stock and sold for just a penny or two. They were very popular and some of us had a whole library of past issues. The most widely read comic was Beano. Others were Eagle, The Dandy, Buster, and Boys Own although that was more of a magazine than a comic. These were what you might call civilian comic books using day-to-day themes of adventure or irreverent put-downs of unpopular adult figures such as strict teachers. Others had a war theme with glamourized portrayals of battles, either imagined or real.

Collecting cigarette cards was very popular among boys and even some adults. These cards were included with the sale of cigarette packages and were a marketing tool to encourage more smoking. The range of themes was huge. Sport stars and teams were perhaps the most popular. Hollywood celebrities were featured. There were even some card sets of an educational nature with subjects such as birds of Great Britain. When the war started, silhouettes and descriptions of aircraft, both friend and foe, were quickly produced. Unfortunately, these had a short life as paper supplies quickly became short.

The collecting of train numbers always seemed a bit pointless to me. This was called 'train spotting' and my friends kept long lists of the numbers of the trains they had seen. Boys would hang out at the railway bridge down by the station to catch sight of the number on the engines that passed under the bridge. Most of the passenger trains were electric and I suppose they had a number on them but there was no glamour associated with the lead locomotive of an electric train as it looked like all the passenger coaches behind it.

The goods trains were usually pulled by steam engines with a metal plate, showing their numbers, so these were a lot more interesting. As they passed under the railway bridge, the road would be immersed in warm steam as if in a thick white fog. If we didn't catch the number as it approached, we would run across the road as it passed under to try and catch its number as it emerged. Fortunately, there was very little traffic on the roads in the war years. This was just as well as two or three boys would rush over the road in the thick steam without a thought that there might be a car coming. Happily, I don't recall any accidents happening while train spotting.

These were just local trains and of a workmanlike nature. If you had the number and name of one of the celebrity steam trains on your spotter list, you had a higher status among collectors. From where we lived, you would have to go to one of the major London stations to see these celebrated trains. At Kings Cross station, if you were lucky, you could see steam locomotives such as The Flying Scotsman on its way to Edinburgh on the LNER line. The GWR line from Paddington to the south and west also had some of the celebrity passenger express trains. These trains were the royalty of the railway system and sights of them were valued by collectors.

Every boy had a stamp collection. Used stamps were carefully stuck into special collector's books with fiddly little hinged sticky bits of paper. When the mail was delivered, each envelope was checked to see if any of them had come from overseas as these would likely have stamps that we did not have in our collections. It seemed that the smaller the foreign country, the more colourful were their stamps. The British stamps with just the king's head on them were very common and dull. On the other hand, we were always looking for an old Victorian stamp called a Penny Black which was reputed to be worth a fortune.

It was possible to buy bags of used stamps from advertisements and other sources. These would contain perhaps 500 or more stamps of assorted origins and values and would provide some fun as we sought to add to our matching series of stamps from different countries. Disappointingly, none of these 'lucky dip' bags ever had any stamps of real value inside them.

Relatives with overseas connections were another good source of stamps. They were beseeched by small boys to save their envelopes and not recycle them in the paper drive bin.

Much care had to be taken when removing a stamp from an envelope. Bowls were often found around the house with torn-off top right corners of envelopes floating in water, waiting for the glue to be softened so the stamp could be easily removed without damage. The stamps were then placed between two pieces of blotting paper and a weight applied to keep the stamps flat when they dried out. Those of us who liked to be considered serious collectors handled the stamps carefully with a pair of tweezers.

Birds' egg collections were to be found in most homes of boys living in the country. These days, it is illegal to take wild birds' eggs from their nests. In Victorian days, this was a popular pastime as you can tell by the display boxes you can still find in antique shops and museums. Stashed away on shelves in our attic at home there were dusty boxes that my ancestors had collected. We had one prized possession, an ostrich egg that sat in a silver display cup.

As egg collectors, we were very conscious that the mother bird would abandon the nest if there was any sign that the nest had been disturbed. We were very careful to gently lift just one egg from the nest without touching the other eggs or the nest itself. We believed that the mother would not miss just the one egg. If we took two or more eggs, she would abandon the nest. I have no idea if there is any truth in that belief but we kept an eye on most nests we found and 9 out of 10 times the remaining eggs eventually hatched successfully. Yet, it was common for various predators to take a heavy toll of the birds' nesting attempts. Magpies, Blue Jays, and various hawks are notorious nest robbers. Cats, stoats, weasels and rats also account for many nesting failures.

Having collected the bird's egg, the delicate part began: the egg had to be 'blown' to get its contents out so that the contents would not go bad. This process consisted of gently holding the egg in one hand while a sharp needle was rotated between the thumb and forefinger of the other hand to act like a very small drill. It was necessary to make a very tiny hole at each end of the egg. Having achieved this, the egg was placed very gently against the lips and, with a big red-faced effort; the filling was forced out of the other hole with a giant breath. It helped to have broken the skin of the yolk so that it could flow out with the rest of the insides.

Beginners were encouraged to practice the process on chicken eggs first as there was a knack to achieving a successful blowing. Chicken eggs were large enough that the neophyte could usually handle the job without breaking the shell. It took a well-practiced person to manipulate delicate small eggs such as those of the sparrow or even smaller bird eggs. It was very disheartening to have got to this last stage only to have the thin shell of the egg disintegrate between your fingers. It would be interesting to surmise the origin of the phrase "To teach your grandmother how to suck eggs". We preferred to blow them.

The final stage in keeping a birds' egg collection was to carefully store the eggs in cotton wool or other soft material in a display box. The real aficionados would finish the job properly by labeling the egg with its common and scientific name.

Even in peace time, playing with toy soldiers was popular. These figures were usually made of lead and painted in the true colours of different regiments. This pastime was not restricted to young boys but many adults, especially retired army officers, created replicas of famous battles by laying out the competing armies in a temporary or even permanent diorama. In war time, this hobby was even more popular.

I was very fortunate to have inherited a modeling set that allowed me to melt down my lead soldiers and re-create them as new soldiers in different moulds. I spent many hours lying on the floor in the living room with the hearth rug rucked up to form an imaginary battleground floor. My collection included some small field guns that could fire short metal rods from their barrels. As I imagined the toy soldiers advancing over the rugged terrain of the hearth rug, I would shoot them with my tiny firearms. It was even possible to load the Lilliputian field guns with percussion caps so that firing them was even more realistic. Tiny packages of these caps were hard to come by and the shopkeepers would ration them out one package per customer at a time to the clamouring boys when news got out that they were in-store.

Inevitably, the impact of the slender rods would cause damage to the toy soldiers. The first injury would usually be the beheading of the enemy infantryman. First-aid was applied by sticking a match down through the neck into the hollow body. A dab of glue was then applied and the hollow head was then stuck onto the top of the protruding match stick. This first-aid would last for a while but eventually the injuries would be beyond repair as my artillery rod-shells would inflict more permanent damage.

With a pile of perhaps half a dozen corpses, I then got out the melting pot and reduced the bodies to molten lead over the living room fire. Once melted, the lead was then poured very carefully into the moulds that came with the kit. There were moulds shaped like soldiers at attention, kneeling and firing a rifle, or lying flat on the ground in a firing position. Other forms were also available, so I was able to create a whole new army from the defeated one.

When I think of it now, it seems that it was a very hazardous job for a ten-year old. Handling lead is now considered a risk, let alone pouring molten lead from a hand-held pot. But that was then and now is now--two worlds apart in many ways--and you could make the case that, in comparison to the other risks of wartime, this soldier manufacturing was a pretty minor one.

Bird watching is a pastime enjoyed by many, both then and now. The bird watching, we enjoyed was somewhat different. We watched for aircraft in the sky rather than birds. In many public places such as the village hall, in the police station and in public shelters, there were posters showing the silhouettes of both Allied and German planes. We were invited to learn to distinguish between enemy and friendly aircraft. While the posters were primarily for the education of air defence people: the air raid wardens, the Home Guard and members of the Observer Corps, they were also of interest to the general public. We studied the posters so that we could identify every plane that we saw in the sky.

You could have called this activity 'plane spotting' but it was more than that. We challenged each other to name not just the type of aircraft but even the updated version of an aircraft. For instance, there were several versions of the famous Supermarine Spitfire since its performance was improved as the war progressed. Some of us claimed to be able to identify the difference between those using the Rolls Royce Merlin engine and the more powerful Rolls Royce Griffon engines or the faster, high-altitude Spitfires with the more pointed wing tip shapes. None of us really knew what we were talking about but it was considered cool to be savvy about such technical matters.

All of these collections consumed much of our free time but the most important collection of all was our treasure trove of shrapnel. Shrapnel could be described as anything that fell out of the sky after a raid. Every boy had at least some souvenirs of the overhead battles. Even if you lived in the heart of the city you could check the roads after a raid. You could go to the nearest park or playing fields and search the ground after a raid. In the lunch hour at school after a raid, boys would spread out over the cricket or soccer grounds hoping to add to their collections. From a distance, you could have been forgiven for thinking they were in deep thought as they ranged over the grounds with heads bowed. In fact, they were searching for that sparkle of torn metal in the grass or a hole in the ground in which they could probe to find this new form of treasure.

Since I was fortunate to live in the country, my area of search was unlimited. I soon had a full array of the more common bric-a-brac that fell from the sky and so became selective for items only of unusual interest I could add to my collection. The occasional brass casing from a 20mm. cannon was always a good find as it had excellent trading value among my schoolmates. Unexploded incendiary bombs were relatively harmless since the explosive device inside was designed to simply ignite the flammable ingredients with a minimum of explosive action. When placed in a vice, the nose section could be unscrewed and the magnesium and carbide powder poured out. After that, the intact bomb casing complete with its aerodynamic fin was in great demand as a harmless souvenir. My older brother made a few pennies by cutting a slot in the upper part of the body to make them into piggy banks.

There was no shortage of supply for these small bombs as it seems many of them failed to explode and burn on impact with the ground. It was not unusual to see small piles of unexploded bombs stacked against the base of the trees or along a hedgerow until such time as the bomb disposal people eventually got around to picking them up. This could take weeks. It all sounds a bit dramatic but these little bombs were relatively harmless if they failed to ignite upon impact. If they did detonate, the flames were not difficult to put out either by covering them with sand or dirt or by pumping water on the flames with a stirrup pump from a bucket of water. That is if they hadn't set fire to a building or corn stack on the farm before we reached them in time to put out the early flames.

Incendiary bombs were dropped from the aircraft in a container we called a "breadbasket". On the way down the large metal holder was designed to open and scatter the many smaller bombs it contained over a wide area. On several occasions, we found the battered remains of these breadbaskets lying in the fields. They were too big to add to my collection and simply went for salvage.

After a raid, it was common to find the fields the next morning littered with strips of silver foil. These strips were about one inch wide and in various lengths ranging from 2 inches to two feet. They had been dropped by the German bombers as foils to break up their images on the radar screens of the defence forces. Since the strips were reflective they created a snowflake effect on those screens and so obscured the 'blips' of the bombers. The Boy Scouts and Girl Guides and other groups were encouraged to gather up the strips and turn them in for re-cycling. We would gather them and roll them up into large balls before handing them in. These reflective silver strips also made good decorations on the Christmas tree.

My pride and joy was a silk cord which I used as a belt for my dressing gown. I found it in a field where a special bomb called a land mine had exploded. This was a bomb that descended on a parachute and landed gently before exploding. It was designed to allow the explosive force to be effective over a wider radius compared to a regular high explosive bomb that buried itself into the ground as it exploded. The crater made by an HE bomb absorbed much of the blast and the area of destruction was therefore reduced. My belt was part of the cord from the parachute that came down with the land mine. Since the bomb was heavy, probably a 500 lbs. monster, the cord was a half inch thick made of a soft silk-like braided material and, therefore, made a great belt. It made for a good conversation piece as well.

Prisoners of War

Before the war, my sister dated a German pilot. He must have been an ace flyer as I believe he competed in the prestigious Schneider Trophy, an air race for seaplanes involving several laps around a course of about 100km. identified by lighthouses and other prominent landmarks. The last such race was held in 1931 and was won by the British Supermarine Spitfire. It was no more than a brief acquaintance but he did fly my sister to Paris in 1938. Of course, the gathering clouds of war brought this relationship to an end in 1939.

This is the only connection with Germany of which I am aware except for my father's WWI experience in the trenches. His association then would not have endeared him to the Germans or them to him, as he was awarded the Military Cross for capturing 12 German soldiers on a night raid into the enemy trenches. In addition, he was the recipient of a German bullet in his leg for his efforts.

Our family name notwithstanding, I don't think we ever had any connections with France. The rivalry between the French and the British has been a long-standing one. The French called Britain 'Perfidious Albion' and the Brits referred to the French as

'Froggies' because of their habit of consuming frogs' legs. This relationship with France and all things French was more a war of words than any true antagonism. After all, no war had been fought between the two countries since 1815 and both countries were allies in the First and Second World Wars.

Despite WWI, it did seem that there was a closer affinity between the English and the Germans than there was between the English and the French. This may have been because the Brits are descended from the Saxons who originally came from what is now Germany. The character of the English is more conservative than the French and somewhat like the phlegmatic nature of the German people. However, the Brits have a better sense of humour. Definitely.

Any affinity that did exist changed as the horrors of Nazi Germany slowly came to light in the 1930's and ended with the declaration of yet another war against our previous adversary. Once again, our allies were the French, our traditional rivals.

When war was declared on September 3rd, 1939, the British propaganda machine leapt into action. Posters appeared overnight with unflattering depictions of Hitler and references to Germans as 'Huns'. This was a term resurrected from the dreadful days of the trench warfare in WWI, and probably derived from the Asiatic tribe that conquered Europe in the 4th and 5th centuries, led by Attila the Hun. The re-characterization of the German people and their leaders had begun.

As a seven-year-old when war was declared, I quickly absorbed the popular opinion of the enemy. With the jingoism of the British attitude, our bravado was mixed with a sense of fear. Every German overnight became evil and their soldiers were monsters out to destroy us all. It was not difficult to conjure up hatred even though the few direct contacts I had later in the war tended to disprove this image.

The first time the reality of an actual enemy appeared in my life was when a German fighter plane was shot down and crashed in the inappropriately named Happy Valley at the south end of the village. This was the first of two planes that crashed there; the second one was British. I believe the German pilot was killed, which at that time didn't concern those who observed the incident but it was not many months before the attitude to the loss of life among our adversaries changed. When a plane, a ship or any vehicle of war was shot down, sunk or disabled, the condition of the occupants became a matter of concern to all regardless of their nationality, friend or foe. Once the threat of danger to the populace was diminished, the bad guys simply became human beings with a soul worth saving.

The remains of that fighter plane were on the side of that valley for all to see. At the earliest opportunity, my pal Richard and I jumped on our beat-up bikes and headed for the crash site. We were not the first to get there as half the village turned out to see this trophy of war. The members of the village Home Guard took their duties very seriously as we were all held back from the downed plane. We could only observe from a safe distance.

However, after the first excitement had died down, a few days later we were able to sneak back to the wreckage, which was then unguarded after the ammunition the valuable instruments had been removed. With much hammering and twisting of metal to and fro, we eventually pedaled home with our trophy. We managed to retrieve a section of the wing or tail that had some of the Luftwaffe markings on it. It became the finest piece in our shrapnel and relics of the war collection.

It was a year or two later before I actually came face to face with a real live enemy combatant. Combatant was not an accurate term implying that the person represents some form of threat. The German servicemen I met were no longer active participants in the war, they were prisoners of war. They no longer represented a threat of any kind. When I heard that some POW's were going to be brought from the nearest prison camp to work on the farm my mind was in turmoil. These men could be dangerous. What if they tried to run away? Would they be chained together or restrained in some way? What would they look like? Would they be fierce and like the pictures of German soldiers on the propaganda posters we saw pasted on the walls?

It was harvest time and they were going to work in the fields alongside our workers. After school that day, I arrived home and asked which fields were being harvested. My mother could tell by my excitement what I had in mind.

Leaping onto the saddle of my newly acquired two-wheeler, but third-hand bike, I headed down the narrow lane and the steep hill towards Shipley Hills. The banks of the lane were covered with the yellow of the spring blooms and sweet fragrance of the wild primroses. But I had no time to notice the beauty of my surroundings. I was at the controls of the very latest Mark 13 Spitfire, the one with the 400 horsepower Merlin engine and the clipped off wing tips which gave it sharper turns and greater maneuverability. The folded cigarette card attached to the frame produced a loud clicking noise which reassured me that I had all the power I needed to take on any plane the Luftwaffe could throw at me.

As I rounded the first bend, a Messerschmitte 109 came at me from the right. As he passed into the crosshairs of my gunsight, I pressed the button on my joystick. "Rat a tat tat", a short burst from my 20 mm. cannon saw smoke burst from his wing tanks. Suddenly behind me, I saw in the rear mirror that I had an enemy fighter on my tail. Quickly pulling back on the stick and with full throttle causing my engine to scream in protest, I swung my steed into a vertical climb. As I completed a full roll in a loop-the-loop, I reversed the situation and came down on him from behind. another burst of gunfire and I caught the pilot by surprise. Two down and a third German fighter changed his mind, having seen my skill as a fighter pilot. He had seen enough and turned for the safety of his home airstrip on the other side of the Channel.

I gave him a few warning shots and he headed over the horizon like a frightened dog with his tail between his legs.

I reached the harvest field and skidded to a stop in a well-rehearsed turn of the front wheel, sending gravel flying. There was no use in using the brake lever as the brake pads were worn down to the metal backing and replacement pads were unavailable at this stage in the war.

As I free-wheeled down the lane to the harvest field, the first thing I saw was a British army canvas-topped lorry. Apart from that everything appeared to be perfectly normal. The old Fordson tractor was pulling the Massey reaper round and round the field, discharging sheaves of wheat every few feet. There were some workers elsewhere in the field gathering up the sheaves of wheat. They were placing them leaning against each other like a tepee with the ears of wheat at the apex. Groups of these leaning sheaves were set in rows of six pairs or so in what were known as "stooks" or "shocks". This was to allow the grain to dry in a day or two with the ears exposed to the air away from the dampness of the ground.

All was normal, or was it? One, two, three, four--there were far more than the normal number of farm workers in the field. Surely, they can't be the POW's working alongside Old Bill and Tom Hogg. Surely there had to be a British soldier standing on guard with his rifle trained on them. But no, there was the British tommy standing by a makeshift table getting the tea ready. And what was that I heard? Could it have been laughter?

This was not what I had expected. These men were the enemy. How could we trust them not to run away? Yes, they were talking to each other in German but every now and then they spoke in English.

Just then the British soldier, the tea maker, called out in English "Tea's up. Come and get it". All six of what I had expected to be fierce, violent men finished stacking the last of their sheaves of wheat and ambled over towards the tea table and towards me. I was not sure what to do but one of them saw me on my bike and shouted to me "Come on son, come and have a cuppa" in his perfect but accented English. Summoning my courage, I laid my bike down and hesitantly approached the group. When I got closer, I realized that they looked just like our own workers only they were a lot younger and fitter. They were not in uniform but in some nondescript trousers and shirts, no prison garb with the arrows all over it like in the Charlie Chaplin silent movies I had seen the previous week at the village hall movie night.

My expectations were shattered. How could this be? They were the enemy and they were here to destroy us. All seemed incredibly normal. They were POW's alright and there was a British soldier guarding them, but his rifle was propped against the army lorry and he was pouring his captives cups of tea while they just sat around relaxing. None of the two or three farm workers were bothered and they, too, sat around but in their own group a little way off, taking a tea break so I presumed it would be OK to come a bit closer.

As I approached the tea table, the guard was slicing some bread buns lengthwise down the middle. A thin smear of oily wartime margarine was applied to the cut side of the two halves of bread which was then followed by a quick wipe of a knife with raspberry jam on it. I recognized that jam as the official version of what raspberry jam was supposed to be. It was the only kind you could buy in the shops. We used to joke that it was some form of red jelly with little wooden  pips carefully inserted to make it look like they were the raspberry seeds. It had a sweet taste but with no more than half a dozen real raspberries per jam jar it was hard to identify what kind of jam it was unless you read the label.

Still, our prisoners were hungry so they lined up by the tea table to get their cup of tea and thick-cut raspberry jam sandwich. As one of the Germans passed by me he held out both hands to the British tommy to take each of the proffered halves of bread. As he did so a wasp, attracted by the jam, settled on one half of the open sandwich. Quick as a flash, the German slapped the other half of the bread down on top of the live wasp.

With a roar of laughter, he exclaimed "Ach, meat ration" in his guttural accent. To my horror, he then took a big bite of his sandwich. The rest of the POW's burst into raucous laughter, the English tommy too.

Apparently, many of the German POW's were quite happy to end up in the British prison camps. Of course, the restrictions and the basic food rations were onerous but, to some, it was preferable to fighting in a war for which they had no stomach. It was not difficult to imagine that a prison camp in England was preferable to facing the unbearable hardships of the Russian front. The practice of allowing the more reliable prisoners to work on local farms was not unusual. It was both helpful for British food production and a popular distraction from the boring life in the camps for the POW's.

Some years after the war ended, I attended a business meeting in Italy where I met the managers of companies from several European countries. There was one fellow there from Austria who had a particularly engaging personality. He happened to speak perfect English without any foreign accent and was keen to know where I came from in England. He seemed to know the place names of towns that I would not have expected to be known by someone who did not live in England. I thought perhaps he had gone to a British university and asked him as such.

"Oh no" he said, "but I did spend four years in Cambridge". It was a cagey reply that was accompanied by a twinkle in his eye. It demanded further explanation.

"Yes", he went on to explain, "I was a guest of His Majesty".

Further probing on my part brought out the rest of the story: he had been a pilot in a German bomber that was shot down early in the war. He and his crew bailed out successfully and duly ended up in a POW camp in the county of Cambridgeshire. He spent four years incarcerated with his fellow prisoners and took the opportunity to learn English. He, too, had worked outside the camp on neighbouring farms. His exposure to farm workers and other civilians had intoned his British accent with just a hint of that part of England. He had no regrets about life as a prisoner and found that the development of his language skills had stood him in good stead after the war.

This was my introduction to the evil Huns who were bombing us by night and were now laughing with us by day. They were depicted in the cartoons as killing babies and showing no mercy as they slaughtered good folk like us. But they were just like ordinary folk, they were just like us. Could this really be true? As news of the atrocities taking place in Europe came to light, it was hard to reconcile these two images, my personal experience and that which the media imposed on myself and others in the village.

This conflicting double image could possibly explain the difference between the usage of the terms "Nazi" and "German". The former referred to Hitler and the type of Germans committing the heinous crimes we were hearing about. The word German was applied to the POW's we came across and for the honourable actions by some of our enemies that were occasionally reported in the newspapers. It was confusing for a ten-year-old to grasp the difference.

"Meat ration" indeed!

A Wartime Diet

When it came to eating well there was a definite advantage to living on a farm during WWII. Like everyone else in Britain, we were issued ration books in 1940, a few weeks after the start of the war. However, the farm, being a primary source of much needed food, provided opportunities to supplement the meagre rations allocated to us.

Initially, food supplies from overseas were reduced but still available. Once the U-boat wolf packs started their devastating toll on the Trans-Atlantic convoys, Britain came close to starvation. The worst period for shipping losses was between June 1940 and February 1941. At one point during this period Britain was within days of running out of food. With a population of 45 million on a small island with an urban population, British agriculture could produce only a part of the nation's food supply. Previous imports of food from Europe dried up as the Nazi forces swept through to France. No longer was it safe for ships carrying supplies to make that short 25 mile crossing of the English Channel.

Ships carrying food supplies from North America, the bread basket of the world, were subject not only to being sunk by the U-boats but also from the pressing need to import fuel and armaments for the British fighting forces. Clearly the ability to defend the country from the threatened invasion from France had to take priority over feeding the British population. Much of the cargo space in the convoys previously devoted to food was diverted to the greater need for fuel and arms.

Food from Commonwealth countries and other world resources was subject to the same danger of Nazi attacks. The greater distances from sources other than North America only increased the danger of ships being sunk. British cargo vessels from the far corners of the world were switched to the shorter Trans-Atlantic voyages.

Access to food supplies was controlled by means of ration books issued to all people young and old, men and women on an equal basis. Some exceptions were made for pregnant women and children with their special needs. Since there were few large chain food stores, purchases were made at the small shops such as the butcher, the baker, the greengrocer etc. It was necessary to register ahead of time with each of your chosen shops so that the owner could apply for the required quantities of rationed goods.

Every visit to a food shop required not only your wallet but also that precious booklet with its tear-out coupons. In a village setting, where food shopping was limited to a few local food stores, the shopkeepers sometimes kept the pertinent pages from your ration book ready for use whenever you popped in. It was not unusual for a housewife to be told "sorry madam but you have used up your coupons for sugar this week". This might or might not be followed with "but maybe I can let you have an ounce or two in advance on next week's coupons". This would always be whispered because there were snitches everywhere, especially in an intimate village setting. In the cities, where there was not the same familiarity with the customers, the ration book was a vital passport to food and was carried by the owner at all times.

There were some variations on the amounts and types of food available with the ration book as the war progressed but very often the stores did not have the supplies available even if you were entitled to purchase them.

In January 1940 food rationing was introduced for bacon, butter and eggs. Each person was limited to 8 ounces of bacon and cheese and one egg per week. As the war progressed these amounts varied and other foods were added to the list until the only items not rationed were vegetables such as cabbages, carrots and potatoes. Even potatoes were rationed for a short time in 1943 when a cold snap of weather froze the '*clamps*' of potatoes stored under straw and earth in the farmers' fields.

Rationing limited what could be purchased but often the availability of foods was a greater limiting factor. Word would soon get around when a new shipment of a scarce and rationed food item was in the shops. It would not be long before the housewives in the village would start to form a queue. Queuing became a way of life for many throughout the war years. It was not without its benefits as it was a great way to meet your neighbours and catch up with local gossip. What's more, it was a good equalizer as, regardless of your social status, you had to be there with your ration books to get your food supplies.

Purchases of bread did not require ration coupons because

of its short shelf life. However, bakers could not sell bread until the day after it was baked. The reason for this was to discourage the excessive consumption of newly baked bread due to its taste appeal when straight from the oven. All bread was required to be baked from a special recipe of '*wholemeal flour*' which was more nutritious and less wasteful than white bread but the taste of the "*National Loaf*" was not popular.

The consumption of fish was not rationed but supplies during the war amounted to only 30% of pre-war levels. Fishing boats were subject to strafing by enemy planes and many of the fishermen had been enlisted in the armed forces. Scarcity was its own form of rationing. Fish and chip shops continued to operate but the oil in which the fish was fried was of sub-standard quality and not always available. Wrapping paper was not available which gave birth to the tradition of eating fish and chips folded in newspaper.

At first a small ration of petrol was allowed but this was discontinued in 1942. A red dye was added to petrol for commercial and farm use. Any private car found using this easily recognized fuel was ordered off the road. The owner incurred an automatic four weeks in jail. Most of the petroleum supplies, particularly aviation fuel, had to be imported by the Atlantic convoys from North America. Access to the British-owned Middle East oil wells was cut off as the Mediterranean was closed to Allied shipping. The convoys of tankers and other merchant ships bringing precious fuel, food and armaments to the fighting forces had to be kept open at all costs. The costs were very high. Some 3,500 merchant ships and 175 Allied warships were sunk during the *Battle of The Atlantic*, as Churchill dubbed this six year conflict. On the German side 783 U-Boats were sunk during this same time period.

Britain produced most of its own coal which was used in manufacturing and for household heating. In the coal producing areas of Britain this form of fuel was readily available but rationing existed in most of the country with quantities calculated to take into account the climate and the season.

Incredible as it may seem, according to government statistics the health of the population actually increased during the war years. Introducing rationing had the side benefit of focussing eating habits on the most nutritional foods. If people had coupons left over they bought and ate the designated food rather than waste the coupons. Since the basic vegetables such as potatoes, cabbage and carrots were often the only foods available after the family coupons were used up, people tended to eat more of this healthy food group. The fact that Britain in 1939 had only recently begun to recover from the hardships and unemployment of the depression years may also have been a contributing factor in showing increasing health benefits despite the food shortages during the war. No statistics are available to support this but it is likely that weight problems for the citizens declined during the war years and for the next decade as food shortages continued long after the war ended.

Restaurants continued to serve the public in a limited way. In order to ensure that the wealthy could not sabotage the rationing system by dining out, restrictions were placed on the menus. Price was one controlling device. A limit of five shillings was the maximum a restaurant could charge for a meal. Prices in nightclubs, special event restaurants and luxury hotels were permitted to be higher. There could be no more than three courses served in restaurants and only one of these could be meat or fish.

To help the working population, municipalities set up a chain of 'utility' restaurants known as *British Restaurants.* By the end of the war there were nearly 3,000 of them throughout Britain. Since the average cost of a meal in one of these restaurants was only 9 pence you can imagine that the quality of the food and service was basic. Nonetheless workers away from their homes were able to get a meal at a reasonable price and with many of their nutritional needs taken care of. I can remember eating in one or two of them. Their *Spotted Dog* (or *Spotted Dick)* steamed dough pudding was very filling but quite tasty if eaten with enough custard. It consisted of a pudding with currants or raisins spotted throughout and a custard sauce poured over it. That and a plate of sausages with mashed potatoes was good value for 9 pence, even if the sausages had more breadcrumbs than meat in them.

The canned processed meat with the brand name *Spam* became a standing joke among diners as the cooks sought ever more creative ways to serve this staple canned meat. It was, and still is, made by the Hormel Food Corporation in the U.S. It contains cooked pork shoulder and other cuts of lesser value meat. If you discount the high quantity of fat in the can it is a tasty and nutritious food easily transported and ready to eat. *Spam* got a bad reputation and was the butt of many derisory jokes because it became a steady diet for the troops everywhere. It was ubiquitous.

Another meat that received a bad reputation among the troops was mutton. Mutton stew became a staple dish on the menus coming from the cookhouse doors wherever troops were encamped. Mutton has a particularly strong flavour and smell when cooked. In the post-war era butchers quickly learned to refer to meat from sheep as lamb, perhaps regardless of the age of the host animal.

Rationing was necessary during the war. But that is not where it ended. It didn't seem to make sense at the time but food and fuel supplies were available even less often in the post-war years and rationing had to continue on for some time. The infrastructure in Britain had been so badly battered and neglected that it took a long time for the infrastructure of the food processing companies, transportation and farming to re-build itself. Added to this, a large supply of food and materials was required to feed and help the millions of displaced persons throughout Europe. There was a real danger of mass starvation post-war as people had to be relocated and provided a living diet before they re-established themselves in a civilian economy. Much of the extra food, fuel and supplies which became available as a result of the cessation of hostilities was diverted to avoid a human catastrophe in Europe. The help that was provided by the Americans no longer found its way to Britain as it was diverted to rebuild the rest of Europe.

Oranges on the Beach

The waves rolled them to and fro on the water's edge. The sun reflected on their orange skins signalling their presence. They were out of place. Oranges belonged in a previous time period and on fruit mongers' counters, not on a pristine sandy beach.

It had been a long time since I had tasted their sweet succulence. I could recall the way we tried to unwind their skins in one continuous piece and the careful way we divided the slices so that we could enjoy them one section, one mouthful at a time. That delayed their consumption too so that the treat could be savoured as long as possible. But that was then and this was now.

Life for some during the war years was a series of disasters. Others like me lived a protected life, aware of the war activities but isolated from the worst of its effects. I was fortunate. There were times when the violence did intrude into my cocooned existence but, for the most part, I lived a sheltered life.

In the spring of 1942, several of us at boarding school developed high temperatures, swollen glands and a lack of energy. We were confined to bed in the school infirmary. It was expected that we would recover in due course as this was probably just one of those maladies that are a part of childhood. As the days went by our conditions did not improve. It was finally thought to be glandular fever or mononucleosis. At that time, there was little the matron could do but to see us through it with lots of rest. But the end of term was coming and no one wanted us to stay on at school during the holidays, least of all us boys.

My parents were informed and my mother took the train from Kent down to Devon to pick me up. The doctor had prescribed more rest and said that perhaps the bracing air of a seaside resort would shake the malaise loose from the grip it had on me. The address book listed an aunt living in Budleigh Salterton near Exmouth in South Devon. The request was made and the invitation to come and stay was received. It was a short train ride from Barnstaple to this seaside resort with a simple change in Exeter. I was bundled up in warm clothing and a blanket for the journey. It was a relief to get out of bed after three weeks but it had left me weak and a little shaky on my feet.

The journey went well and we duly arrived at my aunt's house in Budleigh Salterton. There was to be no more bed rest but lots of fresh sea air and walks on the sea front when my strength had returned. The esplanade ran the length of the curving beach and was an ideal spot to take in the bracing sea breezes. There were red flags and rolls of barbed wire denying us access to the beach itself. Skull and cross bone signs explained that the sands were mined against an enemy invasion yet there was one small strip that had been left open for the local inhabitants to have access to the sea.

That was where the oranges had caught my eye.

I rushed down to the water's edge as fast as my wobbly legs would allow. There were three oranges all perfectly round and plump rolling over and over with each small wave. Quickly, I grabbed them and retraced my steps up the beach, along the esplanade to my aunt's house one street up from the front.

Bursting into the kitchen in my excitement I said, "Look what I've found!" No one was there to hear me.

Wasting no time, I bit into the skin on one of my treasures so that I could start unravelling the peel. Had I been in less of a hurry at that point I might have noticed that something was different. However, my excitement overruled sober thought and I continued peeling back the skin. I wanted to share my find with my aunt so I carefully separated the lobes of the orange and counted out eight perfect portions on to a plate.

The moment had come and I popped the first delicacy into my mouth. This was not the taste I had been expecting. It was impregnated with the salt of the ocean in which it had been floating for days, perhaps weeks. Disappointed, I reluctantly consigned the rest of the oranges to the kitchen waste bin.

At that point, my aunt entered the kitchen with a look of horror on her face. "Where have you been?" was her angry greeting. "Look what you have brought in. It's all through the house. Take off your shoes!"

Glancing down I noticed that I had hard, sticky tar on my shoes.

My aunt was an understanding woman and quickly determined my distress and that I was not aware of the true circumstances of the situation. Quietly, she sat me down and explained that my precious oranges had come from a freighter that had been torpedoed in the western approaches to England and that the oranges had been part of the cargo. The tar on my shoes had come from the fuel oil in the ship's tanks and had washed up on the beach as tar balls where I had innocently stepped in it.

The excitement of the moment had been shattered. It was replaced with long moments of reflective thought about what those oranges had signified. Here I was living a life of relative comfort, giving little thought to what was happening to others. What few inconveniences I faced were nothing compared to the

German U-boats imperiled many a merchant ship bringing supplies over from North America.

sailors who had been on that ship of oranges. It was impossible to tell what fate had befallen them but it was probable that they, too, had been lost at sea like that fruit. My disappointment with the oranges was nothing compared to what had probably transpired for those who lost their lives trying to bring them to me.

I was just an eight-year old boy and could be forgiven for not comprehending the true sacrifices demanded by war. It did open my eyes to reality but eight-year olds live their lives one day at a time. My health returned in due course and I was returned to school to be molded in the manner suitable for a young man. Cricket matches, classroom tests and the give and take with my classmates relegated the oranges incident to a lesser level.

Lesser, yes, but certainly not forgotten these many years later.

Balloon Camp

The heavy rumbling sound was loud enough to wake me up. I liked to sleep in late when it wasn't a school day. I was curled up under the covers dreaming that I was about to score a century for my school in a cricket match against a rival school when my dreams of glory were interrupted by the sound of a heavy engine.

At first, I regarded it as just a nuisance that the farm activity was disturbing my dreams. Then the penny dropped. This was no ordinary sound for a Saturday morning. The vehicle was more than one of the farm tractors. This was something heavier. I prided myself on knowing what was going on at all times in the village. This needed to be checked out.

I leapt out of bed and scrambled to pull on my clothing. Rushing downstairs, I ignored my mother's remonstrations about having some breakfast before I went out. The sound was coming from the meadow beside the house. A heavy engine was revved up and obviously straining. Through the barn, the cattle yard and over the low wall. There it was--a large lorry of a type I had never seen before. It was spinning its wheels in the soft ground. I should have been there earlier so that I could have shown them to veer to the left when they entered though the meadow gate. There was a rocky base on that side where a farm barn had burned down many years before. On the other side there was a shallow pond in the winter but in the dry summer weather it looked like regular meadow grass. No wonder they had got stuck.

How come I didn't know this strange vehicle was coming this morning? Someone should have told me. Over my late breakfast back at the house, I was told that a notice had come in the mail announcing that we were to play host to a Royal Air Force balloon site right there in the meadow. There were two or three other spots they had picked out on the farm for other balloon sites. We had no choice in the matter; it was a War Office decision. These were no ordinary weather balloons; these were barrage balloons that were being deployed on the south and east sides of London to protect the city from Hitler's newest weapon, the V1 or flying bomb.

It was just a month before that we had first seen these new weapons flying overhead at a low height of about 3,000 feet. They were literally unmanned flying bombs with a jet engine on top at the rear and an 1,800 lbs. explosive warhead at the front. They quickly had been dubbed 'doodlebugs' and 'buzz bombs' due to the sound of the engine. They had started to arrive from France and Holland and had taken everyone by surprise. They were Adolf's latest attempt to break the spirit of the British people.

The big lorry finally extricated itself from the soft ground and lumbered up the slope to the one acre site that had been fenced off. A couple of smaller vehicles accompanied it and the unloading began. When the tarps were removed, I saw that the big vehicle had a large winch on its platform with a reel of wire cable attached to it. First, a large spiral anchor was corkscrewed into the

242

ground and the wire cable was threaded through the pulley wheel on the top of the anchor. One of the smaller vehicles was carrying a large grey package which was lifted off the vehicle and unfolded on the ground next to the anchor.

The third lorry carried four folded tents, kitchen equipment, and various household bits and pieces. It was only a matter of a few minutes before the kitchen stove was set up and the kettle was steaming away for the first tea break. The rest of the day was taken up with setting up the tents, digging a latrine, and generally getting the camp set up before nightfall.

Clearly, the four airmen and their equipment were here to stay. I was fascinated by the whole process and observed the entire goings-on from as close a viewing point as the men would allow. These guys were going to live in the open air, cook their own food, sleep in tents, and live a life of which I had always dreamed. I was more than fascinated--I was envious. The fact that they had work to do as well was incidental to me. These lucky guys were on a permanent holiday in my mind. I just wished I could grow up fast and become an airman with a job such as this.

That night, I went to sleep excited to follow the events of the next day. In the morning, I awoke to the sound of another heavy lorry. This time they had taken my advice and turned left through the meadow gate and had no problem reaching the small encampment. This was a tanker lorry. I wasted no time in getting to the site only this time I was told to keep back further for safety. A long pipe was laid out towards the grey mass on the ground and nozzles were attached.

"All smokes out" came the shouted order.

The lorry engine was started up and a quiver was seen under the grey mass. It was alive! The keepers of this living thing straightened out a few folds in the grey fabric. Another shudder or two and the top of the fabric lifted a couple of feet off the ground. A round shape began to appear as the flat mass rose to take its new rotund form. The airmen hustled around like midwives as they unfolded more of the grey material and tied down the restraining ropes. The round body was now clearly visible if a little soft and pudgy. Two appendages flapped like the elephant ears I had seen at the zoo. They were the last to fill out. With a final breath of gas from the tanker, they distended with a pop. Now they resembled the cauliflower ears of a boxer, all puffed up.

The giant elephant was born. A barrage balloon; yet another weapon enlisted to help Britain defend itself against Hitler and his new-fangled machines of war.

The newly-born leviathan was full of energy as the hydrogen gas in its belly strained at the moorings in its eagerness to take off for the beckoning skies. The pumper lorry was shut down and a final check was made of our new baby. All was well; all appendages attached and a fist punch into its belly did little more than wrinkle the fabric for a moment. A birth well handled with a minimum of labour pains.

"You can light up again and someone put the kettle on", said the Flight Sergeant.

It was time for lunch and for the tanker to lumber off to give the breath of life to one or two more balloon babies before the day was done. Just then the rumble of an incoming V1 could be heard headed our way. Flying at just 3,000 feet and at a speed of 400 miles per hour it was clearly visible to the relaxing crew.

"Come over tomorrow and we'll be ready for you" shouted one of the team.

The doodlebug flew on but a few moments later we heard the engine splutter and then die.

"Some poor bugger is going to get a nasty surprise", said the same crew member.

A minute or two later, we heard the "crump" as the V1 crash landed and blew up about four miles away.

Twenty minutes later, we heard the engine of another V1 but this time it was accompanied by the sound of a fighter plane in hot pursuit. At 400 mph, it was a losing battle for the pursuing Hurricane aircraft as its top speed was only in the 300's. With a final hopeful blast of cannon fire, the Hurricane peeled off to the right and went back the way it had come. As the sky began to fill with the wires of more and more balloons, the pilot knew that it was too dangerous to fly any further into the protective zone of the barrage balloons. Not so for the V1 as it flew happily on through the maze of wires unscathed.

When the war ended, I suspect that the War Department judged the zone of barrage balloons as less effective than using anti-aircraft gun batteries in their place. The barrage balloons were credited with only 300 kills. The 40 mm. Bofors guns proved to be the most effective method of bringing down the V1's. Flying at a relatively low height of 2,000 to 4,000 feet, they were within range of these rapid-firing guns. The guns were also more effective than the fighter aircraft as the V1's at 400 mph were faster than most fighters.

The next day, I was up early and high-tailed it to the balloon site as this was the day for the first flight of our friendly jumbo. The crew allowed me into the camp and I went over to see it firsthand. As I approached the fat fellow, I noticed that it had developed a few wrinkles. The air crew explained that the lower temperatures overnight had caused the hydrogen gas to condense a little but, as the sun warmed up the skin, the gas would expand and fill out the wrinkles. I noticed that, up close, the chubby chap had a distinctive smell. Nothing bad and certainly not due to the hydrogen but, as the sun warmed it, the freshly-manufactured rubber-coated fabric gave off an odour of newness somewhat like a brand-new car right off the sales room floor.

Apparently, I was privileged to have got so close. Since the crew were now going to send the balloon up to do its duty for king and country, I was required to be outside the fence surrounding the site. From this position, I was still able to observe the launch. The winch engine was started, the restraining ties were released, and, with a whine of the winch and the cable snaking out, the balloon slowly and then more rapidly ascended to take its place alongside its brothers in the sky that were already up and performing guard duty.

That evening as the sun was setting, I went up to the attic floor of the house, opened the casement window and looked west towards London 25 miles away. The sky was a veritable forest of balloons silhouetted against the setting sun. There must have been 200 balloons in the sky all with their tether wires suspended below them like the stems of forest trees. It was a reassuring sight to see as it appeared that no doodlebug could thread itself through the maze of wires. But it was an illusion as flying bomb after bomb made the journey with just the occasional one being snagged and brought down to earth.

When a V1 did catch a cable two things happened, each potentially dangerous to the people and houses on the ground. The wings of the buzz bomb were made of plywood and were fitted with wire cutters on the leading edges. When contact was made with a tether wire, the cable was cut and the balloon, freed from its anchor, took off for higher altitudes. The buzz bomb had its wing torn off and fell to earth with a loud explosion. Where it crashed was open to chance--a little or a lot of damage could occur. It was for this reason that the ring of balloons was limited to the countryside and kept away from urban centres. In an open field, not much damage would be done but in a built-up area the results were devastating as its 1,800 lbs. warhead exploded.

In the meantime, the severed balloon ascended ever higher until the gas within expanded as the atmosphere grew lighter. Eventually the hydrogen leaked out and the deflated blimp came flapping back to earth. The balloon itself was not much of a hazard but the five thousand feet of wire could cause all manner of damage especially if the cable grounded over some electricity lines.

On rare occasions a balloon would explode in mid-air with a huge burst of flame. The cause was hard to determine; it could have been the result of a German plane taking pot shots at the floating elephants; it could have been a collision with a V1 or perhaps a lightning strike or some other atmospheric ignition. Regulations called for the balloons to be brought down in thunderstorms so lightning strikes were not likely the cause. Regardless of the reason, the balloons were a hazard in themselves and this, combined with their comparatively poor record of kills, raised the question of whether the project was worthwhile.

As far as I was concerned, they were a huge success and I spent as much time as possible hanging out in and around the camp site. I suspect that I was really regarded as a nuisance with all my questions and by getting in the way. As far as the balloon crew were concerned, I think they put up with me for a couple of interesting reasons.

My family treated them well with some of the extras the farm could provide, particularly when it came to food. More than one cake or pie found its way across the meadow. They appreciated the occasional donation of a brace of rabbits, a dozen eggs and veggies from the garden or the farm fields. They became experienced in preparing their own meals with the basic kitchen equipment provided by the R.A.F. A home-made barbecue pit added to their range of culinary opportunities and often sent tempting aromas of roasting meat wafting across the meadow towards our house.

The other reason they tolerated me under their feet was because I indirectly brought them a benefit of a different nature. A large family such as ours generated a lot of clothes to be washed, all of which had to be hung out to dry on the clothesline in full view of their camp site. My 22-year-old sister Pat loved to sunbathe and that summer was often seen in shorts and a summery top. The four lonely guys babysitting the balloon always appreciated a distraction to alleviate the boredom of their job and Pat hanging out the washing was a welcome and lovely break from routine. They were always circumspect in their appreciation but I did hear a few comments among themselves acknowledging that they enjoyed the view.

Every week or so, I was told not to appear on the scene the next day as 'the brass' were coming. Despite their relaxed daily routines, the crew were members of the R.A.F. and therefore subject to military discipline. This meant that they were subjected to formal inspection on a regular basis. The day before the visit by the inspecting officer they scurried around cleaning up the camp site, polishing bits of equipment and making sure the balloon was properly maintained. The next morning, they looked like different people as they stood to attention in their spotless uniforms. A staff car would drive up and an officer would put them through a short inspection. A half hour later the car would drive away, the tea kettle would go back on and the crew would change back into the relaxed fellows I could recognize.

With time on their hands, the crew was able to upgrade their creature comforts. Inside the sleeping tents the government-issue folding cots were soon put away. Instead, the men cut poles from the nearby hedgerow and drove these support legs into the ground to hold aloft a wooden frame with improvised springs made of woven ropes. Bedside tables were fashioned next and other bits and pieces were made to improve their comforts from the natural material in the hedgerow. As I had recently joined the Boy Scouts, I was fascinated by the possibilities of living this open life.

One requirement of the team was to dig four slit trenches to act as foxholes in the event of a direct or near hit on the campsite. Since the V1's were vaguely targeted in the direction of London, it was unlikely that this camp site would receive a direct hit but it was chance that determined where the doodlebugs were going to land. Nothing was certain. There was another campsite on the farm on the way to the valley known as Shipley Hills. They had an identical setup in their camp.

One day a V1 was headed directly for this other location. The crew had heard it coming and probably had it in full sight when the engine cut out. Knowing its flight path, they took no chances and dove into their trenches. The doodlebug actually landed within their one acre site and exploded. All the blast went over the heads of the prone forms in the trenches and swept away all their tents and other paraphernalia but, to everyone's surprise, the winch lorry and the balloon were unscathed. The bomb had landed just beyond the winch and the balloon was 5,000 feet up in the sky. The blast was in one direction only, away from the winch. Sometimes bomb blasts did unpredictable things.

Our balloon crew were an industrious group who liked nothing more than to be busy. When they weren't improving the comforts of their outdoor home or on duty watch for the balloon, they were only too happy to lend a hand on the farm. But they needed to stay within easy reach of their camp site in case of emergencies. Fortunately, the cherry orchard was less than a hundred yards away and overlooked their base.

For the month of July that year, we had a heavy crop of cherries and needed all the help we could get to pick them. Our crew was only too pleased to provide the services of the two men who were not on duty. They were paid by piece work at so much a quart basket of cherries and could eat all the cherries they wanted. As they soon found out, this was not a great benefit as they were satiated with the cherries within the first hour of picking and couldn't bear to eat any more.

The farm had some very tall wooden ladders for picking the top branches of the big mature trees. These 40 foot ladders were heavy to put up against the trees and the strong young backs of the balloon crew were ideal for this chore. From the tops of the cherry trees, they had a good view around the countryside and back to the balloon site. One day, a crew member was picking cherries from the top branches when he heard the sound of a doodlebug coming. It was still a mile away when he saw that it was flying low at about 2,000 feet and it was headed in his direction. He glanced back to see what was happening in the camp site, when, to his horror, he saw that the duty crew had brought the balloon down to top it up with more hydrogen and one of them on the winch was letting the balloon go up again. This was a normal maintenance routine.

The airman noticed that the oncoming V1 was on a direct collision course with the balloon. As the balloon rose on its tether wire it would likely be at the same height of 2,000 feet as the approaching doodlebug. With one more glance towards the camp, he saw that the winch was still sending the balloon up. They had not heard or seen the oncoming V1 due to the sound of the winch motor. Other pickers up the ladders had now noticed the critical situation that was developing. The chorus of warning shouts to the operators of the balloon went unheard over the sound of the winch engine.

The next second the world speed record for descending 40 foot ladders was broken by our cherry-picking hero. Ignoring the rungs of the ladder with his feet and his hands on the outside of the ladder frame he was down in a flash. The audience in the tree tops looked on with increasing horror as the bomb and the balloon continued on a converging course. Our hero broke a second record of sorts as he completed the 100-yard dash towards the camp. At the last moment, the winch operator saw his waving arms, looked up, gulped and threw the winch gears into reverse. The flying bomb came closer. The balloon shuddered with its sudden change in instructions. The balloon started its slow descent. 1,900 feet... 1,800 feet.... 1,700 feet...and the doodlebug passed directly overhead.

From the tree tops came a cheer of appreciation mingled with relief as the danger passed on. The thought of the devastation that could have been caused by a flying bomb with an 1,800 lbs. warhead colliding with a balloon full of hydrogen at only 2,000 feet does not bear thinking about. But it didn't happen and life continued on. It was just one more incident in a war that taught you to expect the unexpected.

As the warm days of summer passed and I continued my love affair with the balloon site, the crew started to call me 'General'. I took this as a sign of familiarity and that I was welcome. I had been accepted, not as one of them exactly, but as a friendly figure as I trotted up to the camp after school to learn about anything interesting that might have happened that day. It wasn't until they had dismantled the site and departed the next spring that someone suggested that my title of General could actually have had a different connotation. That someone, who quickly became my ex-friend, implied that 'General' was just a shortened version of 'General Nuisance'.

I have a horrible feeling that he might have been right.

Friendly Fire

I have never seen any statistics on what is known as loss of life by "friendly fire". If you were to include those who have perished through mistaken action from their own comrades and add on those who died through accidents connected with war time conditions as opposed to enemy action, I believe the figures would be surprisingly high. The process of waging war is extremely chaotic. With the two combatants doing everything they can to outwit each other and consequently taking risks that would never have been acceptable in peace time, the chances of something not going as planned and horribly wrong is inevitably high.

In the trench warfare of WWI there was little concern for the risks for individuals. Strategy was based largely upon the volume of troops that could be thrown into a battle. It was just a question of numbers. The only risk that concerned the generals seemed to be which side came out on top, with the number of casualties simply being a means to an end.

In WWII, I believe more attention was paid to the safety of individuals. More thought was given to what the costs would be in terms of human lives, at least for those on our side. Yes, there were exceptions to this. The raid on Dieppe was an experiment in which little concern was shown for the likelihood of incurring heavy casualties. It was a risk taken with insufficient regard for the possibilities.

But on the whole, the British and American concerns for the safety of our servicemen were taken seriously. Nonetheless, friendly fire and accidents happened at frequent intervals. Our village was witness to two such events. One was truly the result of friendly fire and the other was an unfortunate accident which came about because of unnecessary risk taking by an individual.

The first incident took place right at the beginning of the war. It occurred early in 1940 within a few months of the declaration of war on September 3rd, 1939. It was at a time when people still couldn't quite believe that we were at war. Life had continued on with little change from the routines of peace time except that there was an air of anxiety which had people on edge. It may have been the heightened feelings of the time that caused one pilot to be a little trigger happy and to press the firing button that released a fatal fusillade of 20 mm. cannon fire.

At the south end of our village there was a favourite tobogganing hill. It was known as Happy Valley although as it turned out that was an unfortunate misnomer. At the first sign of any snow, we dragged out the sleds from the barn and hiked the mile or so to this happy place. It was a particularly good location for tobogganing as there was a ridge half way down the slope that gave you a flying lift off for a few feet and always produced screams of delight or groans from the half-frozen sled passengers.

On that early spring day in 1940 it was not a happy place. The R.A.F. was in full action mode training new pilots, many from Commonwealth countries where they had volunteered to help the motherland. Just recently arrived from overseas, these keen but green young men were quickly deep-ended into their military training. In this case, the new recruit was undergoing his flight training in an aircraft that might not have been familiar to this somewhat qualified yet perhaps overly eager fighter pilot.

There had been some German raids over Kent but the heavy bomber formations had yet to be seen. Many of the early enemy sorties had been directed at the British fighter bases such as the one at nearby Biggin Hill airbase. One Sunday, as it was getting dark, the peace of the evening was shattered by the scream of aircraft engines at full throttle followed by the sound of 20 mm. cannon fire. It was not long before we heard the "'crump" of the impact of a plane quickly followed by flames and a pall of smoke rising over the roof tops from our favourite tobogganing hill.

The White Maria ambulance was stationed in our yard. It was just a matter of a few minutes before the emergency crew backed the vehicle out and was speeding south to the scene of the crash. Unfortunately, the rescue attempt was too late--the pilot of the downed plane was killed.

The gossip in the pubs later that week spread the story that this had been a tragic accident involving friendly fire. The dead pilot was believed to have been a Canadian on a training flight. He was reputed to have been shot down by a Polish pilot flying with the R.A.F. in a case of mistaken identity. Some of the Polish air force pilots escaped to Britain when the Nazis overran their country. The Polish pilots had their own squadrons within the R.A.F. and had a reputation for exuberance and a record for bravery in the Battle of Britain.

It was thought that the IFF transponder had not been turned on or was defective in the doomed plane. The IFF stands for Identification Friend or Foe which would have identified the Canadian flyer as a friend if it had been working. Whereas I cannot confirm the facts of this situation, it was certainly the rumour that spread through the village. A limited command of the English language by the Polish pilot may also have been a factor. This incident reflected the tenseness of everyone as this was a time when servicemen and the general public were waiting for the 'real war' to start.

As it turned out Happy Valley continued to be poorly named as later in the war a German fighter was shot down and crashed on the same hill. Two plane crashes in one small valley was just a coincidence but it caused some of us to wonder at the significance of its name.

The other tragic event was a pure accident or perhaps pilot error would be a more correct description. Our farmstead consisted of three different farm sites but all three were worked as one. Each one of the different locations consisted of a cluster of barns and farm buildings.

My brother-in-law was an R.A.F. officer. He had taken flight training but his eyesight was not sharp enough to be a pilot.

He was reported to have damaged more than one training aircraft as he tried to perfect his landing skills. Wisely, he was switched over to the supply side of the air force. He happened to be home on leave when a fellow officer who knew where he lived decided to buzz him in a fighter aircraft while on a routine patrol. No doubt this was against R.A.F. regulations but it was hard to hold down the exuberant twenty-year-olds who were flying these fast fighter planes. Having located where my brother-in-law was spending his leave, this pilot friend started some spectacular aerobatics to get his attention.

Spitfires were very efficient fighting machines and were at least a match for the Luftwaffe Messerschmitt 109's, the equivalent fighter planes on the German side. However, they were not designed for aerobatics and hence had their limitations when pushed to the limit in extreme aerial gymnastics. The pilot of this plane first passed over the house where my brother-in-law was staying and performed a victory role at having located him. He showed off his skill in other aerial manoeuvres and finished off his demonstration with a vertical climb. The point of this exercise is to push the aircraft straight up into the sky and just before gravity takes over and the climb peters out the pilot throws the plane over to the side putting the plane back into a descending glide and normal level flying again.

On this occasion, the pilot missed the point where he should have broken off the manoeuvre. The climb stalled and the plane came tumbling down in a vertical fall. The pilot was unable to break out of that awful spiralling descent. In front of my brother-in-law and the horrified spectators with him, the plane with the pilot still in the cockpit crashed right in the centre of the cattle yard, a mere hundred yards away from my sister and brother-in-law's house. Fortunately, there were no cattle in the yard at the time. It was, of course, fatal for the pilot.

Today, the farm barn has been converted into a house and a swimming pool now marks the point where the aircraft crashed. I am told that a few small pieces of that plane were found sixty years later when the ground was excavated for the construction of that pool.

Casualties from friendly fire and accidents such as this are an unfortunate by-product of the greater risks that are inevitably taken in wartime.

How to Catch a Spy

We schoolboys had a list. If MI5 had bothered to ask us, we could have turned in several spies. We knew they were around. They had to be! Why else would the hoardings down by the station have those posters pasted on them? Along with the posters exhorting us to use Sunlight Soap were the dramatic looking signs telling us that "Loose lips sink ships." There weren't many ships in the village so we felt that one was no concern of ours.

Another poster told us "Adolf is listening." Now that one did apply to us. We were concerned that he knew some of our secrets so we kept quiet every time we passed that poster.

The one that really appealed to us asked "Is your journey really necessary?" That was a very good question as we passed that poster every time we caught the train to school. We agreed with that one. Good question.

My friends and I were loyal British citizens and we found it our duty to watch out for German spies. They could be anywhere around us so we were constantly on the lookout for them. We kept little lists of suspects and compared notes. If the others agreed with our suspicions, those names went on the "to be watched list". This meant that they had to be followed and notes taken on any further unusual acts.

It wasn't difficult to arouse our suspicions. There were certain signs that were sure-fire clues that all spies gave away. We would start with our teachers. Everybody knew that school teaching was a great cover for a spy. Especially teachers at our school in Rochester because that was where the Shorts factory was that built those big flying boat aircraft known as Short Sunderlands. They were used to attack U-boats out in mid-Atlantic and Hitler would want to stop their production. We would see the big lumbering planes taking off from the River Medway when our train to school crossed the bridge over the river. The school was just a mile away from the factory so our teacher-spies could easily report to Adolf what was going on at the factory.

Chatham dockyard was just a mile or two further on down the river and was one of the main naval bases in Britain. We reckoned some of our more suspicious teachers would spend their evenings in the pubs trying to winkle out ship movement information from the sailors and workers at the dockyard. Yes, every teacher had to be a suspect. The women teachers too as there were more of them as the male teachers were called up to go and fight. Lady teachers looked harmless enough but that was the secret of being a good spy.

Some of the other clues that we looked for were somewhat obvious. A German accent was a dead give-away, not that we knew how to recognize one. A French accent was suspicious too as, Allen, one of our gang explained "The French have been conquered by the Nazis and they may have been tortured and sent over to spy on us." But then Allen was a year younger than the rest of us, so what did he know? Nonetheless, we kept a sharp eye open for anyone wearing a beret and smelling of garlic. We didn't find too many.

Anyone wearing a hat pulled well down over his eyes and the collar of his raincoat up around his ears was put on the list. Mick said we had been seeing too many films with characters like that. I don't know…he might have been right.

Beards were suspicious but we made exceptions for any sailors we saw. Moustaches, if they looked like Mr. Hitler's, had to be investigated. Our methods of investigating were very subtle. We would hang out down the road at The Parade where there were a few shops. There was: a newsagent, King the Butcher, a sweet shop, and a grocer's. One of us would lean nonchalantly against a wall pretending to wait for someone. Another one of the gang would be across the road watching for the secret signal from the spy watcher. If he was given the signal, the second member of the team would quietly follow the possible spy to see where he went and what he did. Cool stuff like that.

There was that big house near the village green. It was said that they had television, whatever that was. TV had been invented in the 1930's. They were the only people in the village who had it. The house had big aerials on the roof which meant that they could be communicating with the enemy. They had to be put on the "To be Watched" list because, of the two planes which crashed near the village during the war, both came down in Happy Valley within one mile of the house. There had to be a connection through this special vision device.

After dark was a good time to watch for spies signalling to German aircraft. There were two ways they could do it. Anyone who had not drawn the blackout curtains while there was a light in the house was suspect. If it happened just once then it could have been a mistake, but if it happened a second time and the home owner kept swishing the blinds to and fro they could be conveying information to a passing enemy plane. Anyone with a powerful torch had to be watched carefully. Batteries were hard to get during the war so anyone with a particularly powerful torch was a possible spy.

Sometimes we had to ride our bikes at night and a light was necessary especially on those incredible winter nights when the smog reduced visibility to four or five feet. Since batteries were almost impossible to get, some of us had a 19th century, foul-smelling carbide light. This device dropped water onto a container of calcium carbide that caused acetylene gas to be given off. You had to light the gas with a match and the burning gas gave off a soft light. The carbide lamps were economical and provided light for a long time but they were tricky to operate and the smell was awful. If someone rode by us on their bike with a strong headlamp, they were immediately placed on our suspicious list. After all, if they weren't a spy they would have crummy bike lights like ours.

Our village was in the headlines after the war as a result of the Profumo Affair. This was a spy story of a different sort. Christine Keeler, the principal player in the affair, lived in our village. She was reputed to be the mistress of a soviet spy. She had been sleeping with John Profumo, the Secretary of State for War, supposedly getting secret information through pillow talk to pass on to the Russians. It made headlines in all the newspapers so it must have been true.

So, we were right--our village was a hotbed of spying! My friends and I were right to go spy hunting. There may have been a spy behind every tree and in every bed.

The Tides of War

There were a few times in WWII when the final outcome was in the balance. The Battle of Britain was one; the winter months in 1942, when the U-boats had the upper hand and Britain was close to starvation was another. Then in 1944, when the Allies were clearly in a dominant position, Germany's fortunes were close to being turned around by the introduction of a whole new generation of weapons.

In the spring of 1944, the first of the V1 jet propelled bombs was launched against Britain. The German name for this new weapon was *Vergeltungswaffe 1* but in Britain it was quickly dubbed a V1, a flying bomb, a Doodlebug, or a Buzz Bomb. The last nickname referred to the fact that you could hear this bomb coming in the sky a full minute or two before it reached you. Bombs dropped from aircraft may have produced a screaming sound but only for a second or two before exploding. This new weapon gave you plenty of time to worry about the danger it represented and where it might land. You could hear it coming long before it reached you. You could hear German bomber planes coming but, unless you were in a target area, you could assume they were not going to drop a bomb on you. With the V1 no one was safe anywhere.

267

This advanced warning of danger had a psychological effect on all who heard it. The sound of the engine was a first warning of danger but the threat was heightened even further when the engine sound ceased as this indicated that the bomb had commenced its slow gliding descent. Unless you could actually see the bomb in the sky you had no idea where it would land and explode. At first, this produced a sense of paranoia among the population but over time, with the human capacity to adapt to circumstances, the public learned to interpret the bomb's sounds.

When you first heard the sound coming toward you, you looked up in the hope of seeing it to determine if it truly was coming your way. Doodlebugs flew at a relatively low height of two to four thousand feet and were very visible. They were 27 feet long and 17 feet from wing tip to wing tip. This was the size of a small fighter plane. Once located, you could assess the degree of danger to you based upon its direction as it always flew in a straight line. As it passed overhead, the sound of the engine changed as the jet engine was now expelling its flames towards you as the bomb flew away. You could relax and switch your concern to someone else a mile or two up the line of flight.

If the engine cut out before it reached you and you were unable to see the bomb in the sky, you were well advised to hit the ditch or take whatever shelter was nearby. The doodlebugs flew both by day and by night. In some respects, it was easier to assess the risks in the dark as the flames from the jet engine clearly identified its position better in the night sky.

At the height of the launchings in 1944, over one hundred of these bombs flew over south-east England every day. Each sighting initiated the wailing sound of the air raid warning. Since we lived in the country where we had good visibility, we learned to live with the daily alerts. We became accustomed to hearing the air raid siren followed by the sound of the jet engines as two or three of these Doodlebugs were heard on most days during that summer. On hearing the engine sound, we were able to go out of the house to spot the incoming V1 and decide how dangerous it was for us. It must have been more terrifying for those people in London and in built-up areas as they did not have the clear vision of the sky that we had in open country. If you were unable to see the flying bomb, it made good sense to take cover whenever the engine was heard to stop.

At the same time as the public became accustomed to the daily V1 flights, the defensive forces became more efficient at intercepting them. It was estimated that some 30,000 flying bombs were launched but as many as 60% were destroyed before reaching their targets. The first zone of defence was the anti-aircraft batteries along the coasts of Kent, Essex, and Sussex. With a straight trajectory, it was thought that it would be easy for the standard 3.7-inch mobile anti-aircraft guns to shoot them down, however, the height of the doodlebugs proved to be a problem as they flew at a level just above the range of these light anti-aircraft guns. Heavy duty guns had to be brought in and these plus the newly-invented proximity fuse resulted in about 60% of the V1's being shot down as they crossed the British coast.

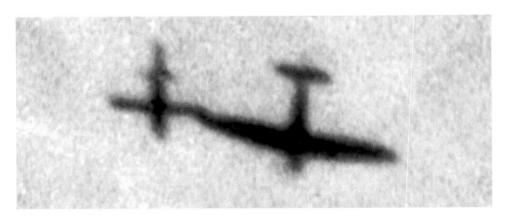

A Royal Air Force pilot tips the wing of a Doodlebug, causing it to crash down, away from a populated area.

The next zone relied on fighter planes. It seemed that the unarmed, straight flying V1's should have been easy targets for the fighter planes. But this was not the case. With a relatively high speed of about 400 mph, the V1's made it difficult for the fighters to catch up with them. The R.A.F. had to station the faster planes like the Tempest, the Mustang, the Mosquito, and the new speedier versions of the Spitfire on the Kent and Sussex airfields to be effective. The best technique for the fighter pilots was to attack the V1's from above as a diving approach gave the slower attack aircraft the extra speed to catch up with their quicker targets. Still, the planes had to be careful not to get too close to the flying bombs at the point of shooting them down. There was always a danger for the fighters if their canons caused the bomb to explode close enough to cripple the plane.

Instead of shooting the V1's down, some pilots saved ammunition by flying alongside them and tipping one of the Doodlebug's wings up with the air flow from the plane's wing causing the flying bomb to descend straight down. This resulted in the V1's being directed to crash and explode in less populated areas. This was a delicate and dangerous manoeuvre but effective because the pilots could pick the time and place where the bomb would fall and do the least damage.

Our farm was located about 25 miles from the centre of London on the edge of the barrage balloon ring around the city. It was interesting to see the fighter aircraft pursuing the doodlebugs right up to the balloon zone, at which point the planes would turn away as they could not fly safely through the forest of wires anchoring the balloons. It was surprising to see how many of the V1's kept going through unscathed. Occasionally one would strike a wire and the relatively flimsy plywood wing of the weapon would be torn off. The bomb would then plunge to earth followed by the usual explosion.

The wings were fitted with wire cutters so the balloon tether wire was sometimes cut and 4,000 feet of wire would come snaking back to earth. The freed balloon ascended ever higher until the hydrogen gas inside burst the balloon fabric in the lighter atmosphere. The deflated balloon came flapping back to earth. All of this created a danger for any houses or people beneath but we could only hope that the risk to lives was less than if the bomb had got through to the crowded streets of London.

For these reasons, the V1's were a psychological success for Germany. The actual damage that they caused and the number of casualties they created was not large compared to the London Blitz but the emotional effect on the British public was substantial. The V1 raids commenced in March 1944 and continued to near the end of the war in 1945 but at a declining rate as the Allied troops overran their launch sites after D-Day.

As it turned out, the V1 was just the first of two terror weapons in the German arsenal. The second weapon, appropriately called the V2, started a second wave of fear in September 1944. The V2 was a 48-foot-high rocket with a 2,200 lbs. explosive head. This was a substantially bigger weapon than the V1 as its explosive payload was 20% more than the V1. It could travel up to 220 miles versus the 180 miles for the V1, and could reach targets further inland or it could be launched from better protected sites further back in Europe.

This placed it within easy range of London and other cities in the UK when fired from launch sites in France, Holland, and even some locations in Germany. Unlike the V1 which was launched from a catapult ramp with a flight path like that of an aircraft, the V2 had a vertical launch trajectory into the upper atmosphere at which point an internal gyro and compass reversed its direction to come down again with a near vertical descent. It arrived at its target without any warning to the local inhabitants going about their daily business. One moment all was well, the next moment they were blown to pieces, never knowing what had hit them.

The V2 was fuelled by liquid gas unlike the V1, which was powered by a jet engine using jet fuel. Both the V1 and the V2 were developed by Wernher von Braun. This German scientist was snatched up by the US military at the war's end to develop the US space program. The first few rockets launched into space by NASA were developed from the prototype of the V2. Von Braun had worked on rocket development for several years beginning in the early thirties.

The Germans had learned that the permanent launch sites for the V1 were exposed to Allied aircraft raids when discovered. As this became a problem, they tried launching the doodlebugs from bomber aircraft. They had some success with this method but lost aircraft and pilots this way. For the V2's, they developed a mobile launch system involving 30 vehicles. They were able to set up this system in ninety minutes and launch a rocket every fifteen minutes. To avoid detection, they then packed up the system and moved on to another location before the Allies could detect the launch site and organize an attack to destroy it.

It is fortunate that von Braun's final success with the V2 rocket came so late in the war. When the V2's were launched, the Allied troops had already started their roll across Europe towards Germany. The end of the war was in sight. The last one to be launched was in March 1945, just three months before VE day.

A total of 5,700 V2's were built with 3,172 actually launched, most of them directed at Britain. They caused the death of 2,500 people and 6,000 wounded. This compares with the V1's of which 30,000 were made with about 10,000 successfully launched against Britain. The V1's caused 6,184 deaths and wounded 18,000. They proved to be more effective in terms of total casualties but the damage caused by an individual V2 was greater than that of a V1.

The closest V2 to land near the farm was about five miles away in the town of Gravesend on the River Thames. It landed near St. George's Square, and destroyed a few houses and killed a number of people.

Part of my father's farm included some marsh land below the sea wall on the Thames Estuary. When we were down there shooting ducks coming in on the evening flight from the North Sea, we could see the exhaust flames from the launching of the V2's on the coast of Holland. Since the rockets were launched vertically into the sky they were visible from where we were some 50 miles away. A streak into the sky was all we could see. From then on, we had no idea where they would come down.

The V2 program was Hitler's desperate attempt to turn the tide against the Allies. But it was too late. If he had been able to use both the V1 and the V2 programs a year earlier, the war's outcome could well have been different.

For Some, "We Had a Good War"

In times of war, relationships tend to be shaken up. Constant change seems to become the norm. Those in the armed services never quite know when the next posting will come through. For the civilian population, the situation is not much different as most people have a job to do whether paid or voluntary. Such activity gets everyone out of their old routines.

Social exposure is increased but the restrictions of movement in wartime ("Is Your Journey Really Necessary?") and the changing war priorities curtail the duration of companionships. The result is that attachments develop more readily but tend to be more short-lived as the whirlpool of the war moves people along in its vortex.

In many ways, this was a good thing as far as British society was concerned: the rigid class system of pre-war days began to break down. This was especially true for the impoverished inner-city dwellers in the major cities and the eastenders of London. Conscription into active military service broke the habits of their former lives for many of the menfolk. For the ladies, there was the chance to discover new capabilities in the women's forces, working in the factories or on the land. Particularly for the children who were evacuated out of the cities into the countryside, it was a new experience. For many youngsters, it was a positive time; for others, less so. Regardless of their experiences, it opened up new horizons.

Many older folks also found their wartime involvements stimulating and their minds and bodies were kept active. Elderly people could find a way to help in the war effort and in so doing create more social interaction and establish a wider circle of  acquaintances and friends. For the senior men, there was pressure to become air raid wardens and firewatchers. Another popular option was to join the Home Guard, commonly referred to as 'Dad's Army'. This gave the older men past call-up age a chance to be useful, and to realize that they were still needed in the defence of their homeland. While their contributions to the war effort were of value, the opportunity to be seen in uniform at church parades on Sundays gave these old warriors a boost in morale and a chance to expand their friendships. An important side benefit was that they could form up outside the church after Sunday service and march straight to the local pub. It was good for them to be seen doing their bit in support of the younger men out there on active duty.

Senior ladies also had the opportunity to get out and enlarge their circle of friends while helping out. The Women's Institute program gave them the chance to meet more of their neighbours but also to break down social strata. There were many other chances for the women to contribute in the many forms of voluntary work. Their traditional role of being care givers was never in more demand. Fundraising for all the worthy causes in war time was an excellent opportunity for more social mixing while helping the war effort.

For many, the presence of foreign troops was quite an eye opener. In the early days of the war, Britons became accustomed to Commonwealth troops and nationals from some of the European countries overrun by Hitler. There was an appreciation that they had come from overseas to help Britain in its hour of need. The newcomers may have looked and sounded different but, in most cases, they shared a common heritage with the British. They were well accepted.

In 1943, the American troops arrived and this was a complete game changer, especially for those residents living near American bases. Their reception by the British public was mixed. On the one hand, they recognized the "Yanks" had arrived to help the war effort but many felt that the US had waited longer than they might have to enter the war. "We've done most of the heavy lifting and now you arrive to take all the glory" was a common attitude. Jealousy of the doughboys' greater wealth and the food and amenities they brought with them was another factor. The more outgoing personality of the typical American contrasted with the conservative and reserved British traits. This contrast was not always accepted, or understood, by either side.

The obvious physical attraction of the American men to British women did not go down well with the British men and some of the British mothers. This was a clear case of jealousy on the part of the British. Of necessity, relationships between American service men and the British womenfolk were fleeting but nonetheless intense. The many instances in which the troops left "calling cards" behind them when they moved on were a further stimulus to the festering sores of envy.

Despite the obvious friction between the troops of the two allies many good relationships did develop. The boatloads of GI brides heading across the Atlantic after the war can attest to this. British families that befriended many of the lonely American service men fostered trans-Atlantic relationships that survived the war. The broadening of everyone's experiences with wartime visitors was in itself a benefit to all the peoples from every country. The world became a smaller and more tolerant place as a result of this exposure.

Yes, social opportunities thrived under wartime conditions. For the wives and mothers, not knowing whether the servicemen would come back alive. In the case of the younger women, not knowing if that bomb had their name on it or if their British boyfriend would come home, uncertainty acted as an aphrodisiac. While not underestimating the genuine horrors and hardships for many, for others WWII provided many chances to indulge in a more social life and become friends with a wide range of people they would not otherwise have met.

It could be said of many that they "Had a Good War", as the popular phrase of the time expressed it.

D-Day: The Invasion of France

The biggest event of the war was the D-Day invasion of the Normandy beaches on June 6, 1944. In 1943 and even earlier, the political left-wing elements in Britain had been agitating to "open a second front" to relieve the pressure on our so-called allies in Russia. Finally, they had their wish and they were right--it forced Hitler to move forces from the eastern front to the west and thus reduced the pressure on the Russian army.

The barrier to staging an earlier Allied invasion was the difficulty of carrying the war to the enemy across the 20 to 100-mile width of the English Channel. In the past, this challenging bit of water was the best defence Britain had. It had steadfastly protected the island nation against invasion for the past 878 years. The last successful invasion of Britain was by William the Conqueror, Duke of Normandy, in 1066. Now the tables were turned. The channel was an obstacle to be overcome by the Allied invasion in the reverse direction on to the same shores from which the Normans had embarked those long years before.

The most recent invasion attempt was in 1805, when Napoleon Bonaparte gathered a fleet of French and Spanish ships to attack England. The British fleet under the command of Horatio Nelson intercepted them off the Spanish coast at the Battle of Trafalgar. As the tall column in Trafalgar Square in London will attest, Admiral Nelson was the victor and Napoleon was unable to reach England's shores.

The only other invasion attempt was by the Spanish, who attempted the same in 1588. The weather was a major factor in 1588 just as it was on D-Day in 1944. King Philip of Spain assembled the large fleet of 130 ships known as the Spanish Armada. For those times, this was a huge show of force not unlike the modern armada in 1944.

His plan was to sail up the English Channel with the Spanish fleet to pick up his army of soldiers along the Belgium and Dutch coasts. With these reinforcements, his intention was to invade Britain and defeat Elizabeth the First. Mary Queen of Scots, a fellow Catholic, had been executed the year before and King Philip of Spain wanted to re-establish Catholicism in Protestant Britain.

His Royal Armada faced the same early setback as the D-Day invasion. The Spanish fleet first set sail in April 1588, but soon ran into a heavy storm that damaged many of the ships, including some of the large fighting galleons. The fleet returned to Spanish ports for repairs. They did not set out again until July 19, some three months later.

The D-Day fleet of 6,319 ships ran into similar conditions. The invasion was planned for June 5th, but the sea conditions were such that General Eisenhower decided to delay the launch as the landing craft delivering the troops could not be unloaded from their mother ships in such rough seas. There was no chance to return to their base ports because the next wave of support troops had already moved into position there awaiting loading for France on Day 2. So, this modern armada had to disperse into the bays and estuaries along the coast of Britain. The big fear was that the invasion fleet might have been spotted and the German forces alerted. Fortunately, this did not happen. Possibly due to the inclement weather.

The conditions were slightly better the next day, but still not ideal. A further cancellation would have meant postponing the invasion for a month when there would be another full moon for good visibility and high tides, which would allow the landing craft to get further up the beaches and to avoid some of the mined defences which would be exposed at low tide, and so the decision was made to risk the marginal weather conditions and go ahead on June 6th.

Back in 1588, the original Armada sailed up the channel towards Belgium and Holland. The massive fleet sailed in a crescent formation, which meant that the smaller British ships under the command of Sir Walter Drake could inflict little damage. However, when the 130 ships of the Armada reached the pick-up points for the troops in Belgium and Holland, they found the ports were too small to provide protection for the whole fleet. Many of the warships anchored off Gravelines, close by modern-day Calais. With his smaller fleet, Drake knew that he could not win against the Spanish crescent formation, but the exposed enemy ships offered him a different opportunity.

Under cover of darkness, Drake floated in eight fire ships among the anchored Spanish fleet. Chaos ensued as the fully laden Spanish ships were unable to weigh anchor and flee before the flaming fire crafts set many of the galleons alight. These were wooden ships with cloth sails, and they were fully loaded with gunpowder. The result was inevitable.

The Spanish ships which did manage to break out were engaged by Drake's waiting fleet. The diminished Spanish flotilla sailed up the North Sea with the intention of rounding the north of Scotland and heading down past Ireland to their home bases in Spain, but their luck was against them. A big storm north of Scotland hammered the Spaniards and many more ships were lost. Another setback was that their food supplies had been stored in crates made of green wood. The moisture in the wood rotted the food and soured the water. It was a fleet of starving sailors in just 67 ships out of the original fleet of 130 that made it back home.

Fortunately, matters went better for the D-Day invasion fleet. Command of the seas and superior air cover enabled the landing troops to establish a bridgehead on the Normandy coast. The bold move to attempt the landing in less than favourable weather conditions caught the German defenders off-guard. The German staff assumed that a landing would not be attempted in such adverse conditions. The commanding German General, Field Marshall Irwin Rommel, was away from his area of command celebrating his wife's birthday back in Germany.

On the first day, about 175,000 men were landed and established a small bridgehead. This was achieved with total losses of about 2,500 troops spread over the four beachheads. By the end of the month, fatal casualties had mounted to 10,000 but this was less than the losses that Churchill had expected. Still, the landed troops did not achieve the advances hoped for.

It was not until the end of the month that the invasion troops were able to break through the German Fifth Panzer Army to reach Caen and Bayeux where they could create a bridgehead large enough to be secure. It was important to have a bridgehead that would enable supplies and reinforcements to be landed out of range of the German forces. By July 4th, one million troops had been transported to Normandy with huge quantities of vehicles and supplies.

The invasion fleet set sail from south coast ports from Chichester to Plymouth with Portsmouth as the principal command point. This was a long way west from where we lived in North Kent, so we did not see the huge build-up of troops on land and the warships at sea, however, the sense of anticipation was felt throughout Britain. Everyone knew an attempted invasion was inevitable; it was just a matter of when and where.

In the meantime, the daily flights of the V1's and V2's continued. These new weapons were effective in causing damage and casualties, but the greater impact was the raised stress levels for residents in the south and eastern counties. The war was going well for the Allies with the battle for Italy; nevertheless, Hitler's new weapons created a setback for morale in Britain. A successful invasion of France would not only be a boost for public spirits, but eventually result in the Allies overrunning the launch sites for these unmanned bombs from the sky.

Very early in the morning of June 6th, I awoke to the rumble of aircraft flying overhead. That was not unusual. By 1944 daylight raids by our bombers into occupied Europe were more frequent. But this time the throaty roar of the planes was different and louder than usual. Rushing to the back door and out into the yard, I was astonished to see aircraft from horizon to horizon.

These were not just the usual bomber formations; these were units of two aircraft, one behind the other and in close proximity. From the ground, I could not see the towlines, but quickly determined that these were planes towing gliders. I knew the silhouette of just about all makes of aircraft, both our own and those of the enemy, but I had never seen these snub-nosed flying

Troop Glider on a tow-line, filled with anxious troops.

machines that had no engines. I recognized many of the tow planes as Dakotas, the work horses of the Allied Air Forces, but I could not name the gliders on the end of their leashes.

Like many boys of my age, I had a well-thumbed copy of Jane's Book of Aircraft Recognition, so I quickly checked and found that these were Airspeed Horse gliders, each capable of carrying 28 troops. These silent-flying aircraft had a distinctive look as the nose of the plane looked like the head of a grasshopper with its flat front. Although I am sure there were fighter aircraft in the vicinity to protect them, these planes had no means of defence or more than basic manoeuvrability. They were simply passenger vehicles or buses to take troops from A to B.

All gliders were extremely vulnerable in the air and even more so when landing as they were expected to come down wherever they could find some level ground. Nonetheless, war records show that most gliders reached their landing zones successfully during the invasion. Once landed, their working life was over. The troops from the gliders played a major role in capturing the Operation Pegasus targets of strategically important bridges behind enemy lines.

This was a Tuesday morning, a school day. My parents had come out to see what was going on and we stood together in the yard with hearts thumping with the enormity of the spectacle. The night sky was disappearing to the west as the first rays of dawn were beginning to light the scene from the east. The light of dawn reached the planes in the air before it arrived on the ground. The warriors in the sky did indeed seem like knights in shining armour against the darkness of the departing night.

The time was about 5:30 in the morning and my train to school left the station at 8:15, so there was plenty of time to get ready for school. But there was no question of my going to school that day. Even if my parents had insisted, I would have played truant.

The sight of such an aerial armada brought a peculiar complexity of emotions. The excitement of what was obviously the start of the much-anticipated invasion was uppermost, but mixed in with the excitement was pride in what our country was about to undertake leavened by anxiety for the thousands of troops that were passing overhead on their way to danger and an unknown outcome. We knew that there were rows of battle-ready men up there in each glider, each deep in his own thoughts, undoubtedly experiencing anxiety, even outright fear, for what was about to come. Our thoughts were with them.

The scene of all those troops headed for their engagement with the enemy soldiers must have been especially poignant for my father who had faced the same anxious moments many times in the trenches of WWI. He had led his platoon "over the top" and he knew the fear, the risks, and the horror that awaited these young men in the sky. He even had the physical scars to remind him of that hell.

As the hours continued, more and more flights of the glider units passed by. They had come from the major airfields in East

Anglia to our north. The flight path to their landing grounds in France took them directly overhead. I had started counting from my first sight of them, but, as the numbers reached 500...600...700, I finally gave up. The sky was still filled from horizon to horizon. There were too many to count. Let's just say they were in the thousands.

Eventually, we returned indoors for some breakfast and turned on the radio only to be told what we already knew. This was indeed the start of the invasion. As we ate our breakfast, we realized that those first gliders we had seen must have since landed and the battle was on. We could only wish them good luck.

As the day wore on we followed the invasion from what we could observe. It was too early to get any details from the radio because the progress had to remain confidential for fear of aiding the enemy. Even in north Kent, which is about 40 miles north of the English Channel, we could hear the deep rumble of the big guns of the warships pounding the German defences. There was a lull in the overhead flights until early afternoon when waves of heavy bomber formations passed overhead on their specialized missions.

Somewhere up there in the sky, there were other transport aircraft carrying troops who were destined to parachute behind enemy lines. There were so many planes passing overhead even my keen and knowledgeable eye was not able to distinguish the purpose of all the various aircraft in the traffic above. Apparently, some 18,000 Allied paratroopers landed on D-Day itself. Many of them were in the aerial traffic that filled the firmaments that day.

Some of the Dakota tow planes which had dropped their gliders off just short of their target areas were seen retracing their steps back home. Later, those planes with more glider partners were seen again passing overhead, but not in such huge numbers. One could only wonder how many of them made it back safely as they were not much more than slow tractors pulling passenger wagons and would have been quite susceptible to enemy attack.

Even as the full force of the invasion team was unleashed on the enemy, Hitler was able to retaliate with his new weapons. As the massive air formations passed overhead, a lone doodlebug passed along a flight path at right angles to the invasion forces, but several thousand feet lower. This V1 was headed in the direction of London, but it no longer seemed to carry the same threat as it had done the day before. It was such a puny response to the big act now taking place that it was almost laughable. No more did it carry the same psychological impact it once had. Of course, it was no laughing matter for whoever might have been near its final impact point. One could only hope that it landed where no damage occurred or lives were lost.

Then we noticed that we had missed something while our eyes were focused high in the sky overhead: our balloon team in the nearby meadow had hauled down their jumbo and it was straining at its leashes at ground level. A further glance around showed that there wasn't a balloon in the sky anywhere. Instructions had been phoned around to lower all barrage balloons while the big aerial armada was on its way to France. This also meant that, for the moment, the doodlebugs had a free pass on their way to their targets.

Now that the big day had come and gone, life for us returned to some form of normalcy. I had to go back to school and homework assignments still had to be handed in. Some of the tenseness of the pre-invasion days had been replaced with the excitement of the new turn of events. Every newscast was listened to for even the least bit of news from France. Success was not guaranteed and, after some weeks, the invasion seemed to have stalled. In fact, there were some anxious weeks in December and January when the Germans mounted a counter attack through the forests of the Ardennes. This halted the Allied advance until the American forces broke the German thrust into the Allied lines in what became known as the Battle of the Bulge.

When Paris was finally liberated in August 1944, it had seemed only a matter of time before the final goal would be achieved. However, on the home front, the V1 and V2 attacks continued until the last raids in March 1945. There was relief that the war was finally being taken to the enemy back on European soil, but, at the same time, the V1 and V2 raids had intensified.

Now our worries switched to hoping that the troops still undergoing fierce fighting would survive unscathed. Who would have the bad luck to be the last person killed before the peace whistle was finally blown? Someone had to be that last victim. Every family with connections to a loved one still in active combat, hoped that they would make it unharmed right up to the day they would all come home.

As the soldiers in their landing craft and the paratroopers in their transport planes left the shores of England behind for the unknown that lay ahead, the songs of Vera Lynn, the "Forces' Sweetheart", were there to remind them what they were fighting for and to give them the resolve to see it through for loved ones and country.

The lyrics of Lynn's "There'll Be Bluebirds Over the White Cliffs of Dover" which speak of "love and laughter, and peace ever after, tomorrow when the world is free" and her hit "We'll Meet Again... don't know where, don't know when" conjured up thoughts of hope and home and the end of the war in everyone's hearts.

Nasty Things Did Happen

Yes, nasty things did happen and not all the combatants behaved like gentleman. The German pilot who decided to drop in on us in the harvest field may have been an exception. He showed good manners and respect for the innocence of the people who unwittingly became his captors. There were many others on the side of the "Bad Guys" whose actions were despicable. I cannot vouch for the "Good Guys" side as I did not witness any negative incidents, but you can be sure that not all of our team wore halos.

There was the case of the German fighter pilot who decided to use some of the farm workers for target practice as if he was on a shooting range. It was haying time in June when two elderly workers and a Land Girl were loading a tractor-drawn hay wagon from the rows of cut and dried hay in the field. The girl was driving the tractor; one man was using his pitch fork to pass the loose hay up on to the wagon. This was before the day of automatic machines that baled the hay in the field. The other old fellow was distributing the loose hay on the wagon to make sure it didn't slide off on the steep slope down to the yard. It was a full load and ready to be taken down to where the haystack was being built by the winter cattle yard.

It was an idyllic country scene reminiscent of a Constable painting. All was innocent, peaceful, and bucolic. Suddenly, out of the calm blue of the sky, a single German fighter aircraft, "hedge hopping" to avoid radar detection, came down the valley known as Shipley Hills. Everyone was taken by surprise. One moment the farm workers were chatting quietly amongst themselves as they moved slowly down the neat row of winnowed hay. The next second the roar of the aircraft's engine shattered the stillness of the moment as the war machine burst over the nearest hedge at a branch-trimming height.

The pilot, too, must have been surprised because you can't see far ahead at that low height. The picture that so quickly came into view was that scene of peaceful country life featuring the two ancients and the girl. They could hardly have been considered a legitimate enemy target. An honourable pilot would have passed on by in his fast-flying, death-dealing war chariot. But this was no honourable pilot.

Banking steeply, the pilot did a 180 degree turn and came back with his machine guns blazing to shoot up these old folks and the girl. Fortunately, the threesome saw what he had in mind as it took him a minute or so to get into a strafing position. With creaking backs, the old fellows moved faster than they had done in ages, pulling the girl under the wagon with them. Luckily, the hay wagon was full. The ten foot height of loaded hay and the two inch thick oak boards of the floor of the wagon were sufficient protection for them.

This incident had a happy ending as no one was hurt and, on the flip side, probably earned the victims an extra pint or two at the pub that night. Still, it said a lot about the mindset of a pilot that would go out of his way to try and kill such blameless people.

In contrast to this instinct to kill for no good reason, an event occurred which presented the opposing state of mind on the part of a German flyer. It was told to me recently by an acquaintance who still recalls the incident clearly. June was about four years old at the time. She was living with her parents in a beachside cottage in Sizewell on the coast of Suffolk. The flat lands of East Anglia were ideal for the construction of airfields. Many of the US and British bomber bases were located there. Since Suffolk borders on the North Sea, the bomber formations also had reduced flying time for their raids on Germany.

June loved the village and beach location where she could run free with few restrictions. One day, some army personnel turned up at her parent's door and said the family had to move because they were going to mine the shoreline and their house would be in the middle of the minefield. Accordingly, June's parents had to relocate. After one or two temporary moves, they ended up renting a cottage just two fields away from the US air base at Parham. They were so close that June could see the bomber pilots through their cockpit canopies as they took off and landed.

On one occasion, June and her brother were at an upstairs window during an air raid. This was not the wisest place for them to be at that time, but the curiosity of youth overcame prudence.

It was a summer's day and the window was wide open. The two children had their heads out of the window so that they could see better what was happening. All of a sudden, they noticed a German light bomber coming towards them flying very low. The plane was hedge hopping to avoid detection by the base radar system.

As the German plane passed close by them, they could see the pilot inside the cockpit. In turn, the pilot could see the two children leaning out of the window. As he flashed by, he turned his head in their direction with a smile on his face and gave them a friendly wave. The naive children waved back at him. The German flew on intent on bombing and strafing the US air base just two fields away. That was the last gesture the pilot ever made--a minute later his plane received a direct hit and he was killed.

Unlike the pilot that went out of his way to strafe the old men and the girl in the hay field, this pilot was simply doing his duty in attacking a legitimate target, the US air base. This was just part of his responsibility as an enemy combatant. That he made the friendly gesture to the two children is a credit to his humanity.

The image of this scene has stayed with June ever since. However much she may condemn the evil acts of the Nazis, she has retained a softness in her heart for this pilot and the brief gesture of the human condition he showed before his sudden death. It is small moments such as this which tend to outlast the bigger memory of the faceless nature of the war in its enormity.

Nasty is perhaps too mild a word to describe another vicious practice that was observed on more than one occasion during the crucial months of the Battle of Britain in 1940. At that time, the Allies were desperately short of experienced pilots. In the short period from July to the following October, precisely 1,547 Allied planes were destroyed and 966 aircrew were either killed or injured. The crew members that did survive were exhausted from the frequent sorties being flown. After a brief respite, they returned to the sky to continue the fight.

It seems that the German command encouraged their pilots to strafe their Allied counterparts who bailed out successfully. By returning safely to earth on their parachutes, pilots were likely to fly again in new aircraft. Strafing these floating aviators was a strategy to further reduce the supply of flyers for the Allied forces. No doubt many of the German pilots were reluctant to follow through on such an order for chivalrous reasons, but there were some who were not so chivalrous. On more than one occasion, we observed a German plane deliberately targeting the helpless figure of a parachutist descending to earth. At a height of a few thousand feet it was not possible to determine how successful such shootings were, but the attacks could be seen from ground level.

Just as sickening were those occasions when a pilot of either allegiance managed to bail out of his plane only to find that some of the burning fuel from the downed aircraft had ignited his parachute. With over 4,000 aircraft of both sides being shot down in the four-month period of the Battle of Britain, more than 30 aircrew members each day had to try to make that hazardous descent by parachute to safety. With such odds, unfortunate accidents were bound to happen. Our hearts and prayers went out to the victims regardless of their nationality.

Big Ben, chiming throughout the War.

The London Blitz was a devastating event, cruel beyond measure for those citizens who were unable to escape the city. At 4:00 pm. on September 7, 1940 the first wave of 1,000 German bombers and fighters, guided by the River Thames, appeared in the skies above the city. Prior to this date, Britons were accustomed to the daily raids on the R.A.F. airfields that left London relatively untouched. Now Hitler had decreed that it was time to take the war to its citizens.

The first raid continued for two hours as formation after formation of German bombers, with engines growling with the weight of their payloads, carpet bombed the age-old city. The devastation and the flames from their incendiary bombs illuminated London well into the night. Before midnight, a second wave of raiders pummelled the city again until 4:00 in the morning. They were aided by the fires set by the first attack. It was in this raid that both the Houses of Parliament and Buckingham Palace were hit.

For the next 57 days, the German bombers returned every single day. This was strategic firebombing designed to break the spirit of the British people. In this, it failed as it built up the nation's resolve rather than breaking it down.

Other cities were hit as well, with the worst devastation in the city of Coventry. All told, some 40,000 people were killed in the period between September 7, 1940 and the following May, when Hitler called off the blitz and diverted his bombers to the Russian front.

The London Blitz was visible from the farm. The east end of London around the docks was about 20 miles away. From a high point in the meadow, we could see the fire storm created by the mass bombing. Wave after wave of bombers passed over us with a steady grind of the engines of the planes with their bomb bays full. The tone of their engines on the way back had a different, lighter sound. This was a terrible and awe-inspiring time. I can say only that I was fortunate to have been only a spectator to this indecency and our hearts went out to those people we could only imagine facing death under those flames.

These were just some of the ugly events of the war to which we had some exposure. Some would say that the Allied bombing of Dresden, Munich, and other German cities later in the war were just as reprehensible and went beyond the level of civilized conduct in war. The leaders on both sides of the conflict may be held to account for these mass atrocities, but not the participants. My greater concern was with the individual fighting men who chose to perform despicable acts on their own volition.

All war is horrible. There are some who choose to make it even more so. Likewise, there are some combatants who are able to retain a measure of human decency despite the nastiness of it all.

The Grey Years

VE Day, Victory in Europe Day, finally arrived on May 8, 1945. As expected, the population went wild. It would have been fun to hop on the train and join the celebrants in London's Trafalgar Square, but my parents forbade their 12-year-old child to go. Instead, those of us who were at home headed for Woodlands Park in nearby Gravesend. A huge bonfire had been quickly assembled. There was plenty of fuel around with many homes in the town destroyed by the German bombing. The pile of lumber and the detritus of war was the height of a two-storey house before the match was applied. It burned for the best part of a week and the partying lasted almost as long.

My friend Richard and I joined the thousands of celebrants. It was a night to remember as the singing, dancing, and drinking of a happy, thankful, and, in some cases, melancholy populous unloaded the stress of six years of war. It was a good time to wear a uniform as you were everybody's hero even if you had only pushed a pen behind a desk throughout the war. Even the old codgers, dressed in their Home Guard uniforms, got a thank-you kiss from the girls.

This was the end of the dark years of war, but it was only the beginning of what I have called the Grey Years. The war in Europe was over and it was a great relief to know that the killing had finished, but when the hangovers were slept off the next day, little had changed in economic terms. Food rationing was to continue for another nine years, although little by little some restrictions were relaxed. The grime and the long shadow of war was everywhere. The historic and handsome buildings in London were battered from the Nazi bombs and grey with neglect. Nothing had been painted in six years. The stone surfaces of London's monuments were grey from the dust in the air and the breath-denying smogs. The burning of coal in the millions of homes of the city created a toxic mix of fog, smoke, car exhaust fumes, and industrial pollution.

The smog was at its worst in the first half of the decade of the fifties. Visibility in the dark winter months, particularly in November, was so poor that there were frequent occasions when a passenger in a car would have to get out and walk along the curb with a torch directed back at the driver while he drove at no more than walking pace. It was reminiscent of the early days of motor cars when a servant was required to walk ahead of the new-fangled automobiles with a warning flag held aloft. In those days, the speed limit was ten miles per hour, but, in the 1950's, you were lucky if you could cover three miles per hour in that thick, choking smog.

It was a terrible time for those with breathing problems. Each night when I took off my shirt, the inside of the collar was black with the soot, the tar, and the smoke. It was not until regular coal fires in the homes were banned that the smog began to lessen. For home heating, householders were allowed to burn only anthracite or coke. Both of these forms of coal had fewer impurities such as tar and sulphur, and so were cleaner burning fuels. It was not until 1951, six years after the end of the war, that Britain got a grip on itself and made a big effort to smarten up and look forward again with some of the old spirit. The inspiration for this came with the Festival of Britain. For months leading up to the Festival, every important building in the major cities had been steam cleaned, removing the grey coating of neglect, smog, and coal dust. Window boxes filled with flowers appeared on building faces. Flags sprouted like spring flowers after the rain. Britain was treated to a good old "wash and brush up", to use a Cockney phrase.

Every village and town in the country joined in to celebrate this rebirth. Street parties were held everywhere. Flags festooned even the modest of streets. Parades and floats wound their way down every community's main street, including ours. Musical instruments were taken out of hall cupboards, dusted off, and their sounds were added to the joyous melodies of local bands. All were welcomed in the parades even if the players had more enthusiasm than musical talent.

After the parades, trestle tables were brought out into the centre of the High Streets and placed end to end down the faded centre line of the roads. All traffic was banished until the festivities were over. Tablecloths printed with the red, white, and blue of the Union Jack were spread on the bare table boards. Mounds of food and beer came out of every home. Front parlour chairs saw the light of day for the first time in years and everyone sat down to a home-grown feast and general booze up.

Spirits were given a lift with the Festival, but still the hard times and rationing continued for several more years. Services and consumer goods remained in short supply. There was a phrase that was heard frequently to explain why something was not available or couldn't be done: "We've had a war, y'er know!" was the excuse for any incompetence or reason why someone was unable to provide good service. It became a universal catchphrase and belonged right alongside the national trait of 'whinging'. This was a combination of whining and complaining. If something could not be done or provided, the next phrase you would hear was a throwback to the government posters of 1940 when the populous was urged to "make do and mend."

No, the Grey Years were not one of Britain's finest times. They persisted up to the 1960's, when a new generation of young people turned Britain into a world leader in lifestyle, fashion, and fun. London became the place of the "Swinging Sixties" but that was to come later. In the meantime, Britain dragged itself through the smoggy and depressing postwar years. However, there was light at the end of the tunnel and the strength of the British people would win through. The phrase: "that's the spirit" sums up the attitude that made it all happen.

On the farm, the two cars were suffering from six years of overuse and too little care. They were patched up as best the local garage could manage. My father put his name down on a waiting list for a new car. Two years later, he managed to buy one so long as he was prepared to accept the only make available. He ended up with a Humber Hawk. This car served its purpose, but was over-priced and a tad gutless. Never mind--it was a new car and anything new was good.

Older vehicles in reasonable condition were fetching high prices. Through a personal friend who was a car dealer, my mother managed to get wheels of her own. One day she drove into the yard grinning from ear to ear behind the wheel of a British racing green convertible 1937 Sunbeam Talbot Grand Turing model with an engine in front that was six feet long. It was an impressive car and far too powerful for my mother, who really only needed a small vehicle for shopping and puttering about. Since I had just passed my driving test, I persuaded her that she would be safer in the old clapped-out Hillman Minx that was still roadworthy, but only just. That Grand Turing model was the vehicle that I drove to the Lake District for a holiday with my girlfriend a few years later. The impressive car and the fabulous scenery might have been the real reason I returned home with my future wife, Barbara, by my side. I have to thank that car for more than its physical performance! But I have leapt ahead.

The end of the war in 1945 found me still at school in Rochester. My parents felt that another spell at a boarding school would do me good now that the anxieties of the war were over. Two of my older brothers had gone to school at Malvern College and I was to follow.

The only thing was that there was no Malvern College or at least not in Malvern, Worcestershire. The school had been requisitioned in 1939 for the development of radar and the boffins had not yet left the premises. As such, the school was taken in on a temporary basis by Harrow School near London. That's where I ended up for the first couple of terms before we all moved back to Malvern and to school grounds that needed a lot of reclamation. One of the first activities included swinging sledge hammers to knock down the temporary brick buildings the radar people had put up. What with turning sheep pastures into playing fields at my first school in 1940 and studying a course in deconstruction at Malvern, my education had included its fair share of the physical sciences. Both were results of the government's poster urging us to make do and mend.

School life at Malvern College was pleasant enough but I suspect that my scholastic studies might have been more advanced if I had stayed at Kings School, Rochester. It took a few years to re-build both the grounds and the teaching program at Malvern whereas there had been no serious interruption to the education program at Rochester.

Leaving school at the age of 17, I obtained a job in London in 1949. I was biding my time before my call-up for compulsory national service at age 18. I worked at the foot of the Haymarket for the Orient Line, the shipping company that plied passenger liners between the UK and the Far East. My job was in the Passenger Department, booking cabins for the travelling public. For this, I was paid the princely sum of £150 per year.

Knowing that my two-year military service would probably find me square bashing and painting stones white in some army camp, I decided to find a way to be drafted into the Navy. To achieve this, I joined the RNVR as an Ordinary Seaman and attended HMS President on the London Embankment every Tuesday evening. A cruise for two weeks in an old wooden mine sweeper from London to Edinburgh and across to Norway was the highlight of that summer. This extra effort paid off and I was duly conscripted into the Royal Navy in 1950.

After the usual new recruit indoctrination, I was fortunate to enter the navy's upper yardman program. This led to an intensive training program aboard a battleship and then an aircraft carrier. Graduating as a Midshipman, I was pleased to be assigned to a destroyer and spent the next year cruising the Mediterranean at Her Majesty's pleasure. It was at that time when the Korean War started. Pressure was applied for me to sign on for longer and go to Korean waters. Instead, I chose to stay with the short-term assignment and enjoyed my Mediterranean tour.

During the Grey Years, I was fortunate to spend over a year away from the dreariness of life in England. I returned to civilian life and was taken on as a trainee by a timber importing company in London. It was not long before the smog, the boredom of the trainee's role, and the depressing conditions in the London of 1954 caused me to look further afield. This was not surprising after basking in the sun and the blue waters of the Med. for the last year or so.

In April 1954, I boarded a Canadian Pacific liner and set sail for Canada. The war years and their aftermath were a thing of the past, and this war brat was off to a new life.

About the Author

The author, Derek French, is shown here (left) enjoying one of the few beaches in England that was open to the public during World War Two. Most beaches were mined with explosives as a defence against possible invasion with just a small section left open for the public to enjoy. After the war, he emigrated to Canada with his new wife, Bobbie, where they still reside today.

If you wish to get in touch with Derek, you can reach him at derek.french475@gmail.com.

If you wish to order another copy of this novel online, you can do so through Amazon.

19887988R00181

Printed in Great Britain
by Amazon